Lord of the Rings

From Singleness to a

Successful Marriage

DRS. MATTHEW & LATASHA NESBITT

DR. NES INTERNATIONAL CONSULTING & PUBLISHING

PASADENA, CA   LOS ANGELES, CA

Dr. Nes International Consulting & Publishing

P.O. Box 70167

Pasadena, CA 91117

www.drnesintl.com

The book recounts certain events in the life Drs. Matthew & LaTasha Nesbitt according to their recollection and perspective. The purpose of this book is not to defame, but to empower and motivate readers to pursue successful relationships.

ISBN: 9780999178539

Senior Editor: Femi Fletcher

Cover Design: Gift of Graphics

DEDICATION

For your desire to learn and grow, may your (future) relationships expand in ways unknown.

All blank pages are intentional

Table of Contents

Introduction 7

CHAPTER 1: SINGLENESS.. 11
HERS 11
HIS 26
MIRROR MOMENTS 39

CHAPTER 2: DATING 45
HERS 45
HIS 56
MIRROR MOMENTS 74

CHAPTER 3: ENGAGEMENT 79
HERS 79
HIS 90
MIRROR MOMENTS 100

CHAPTER 4: MARRIAGE 105
KEY AREAS OF DISCUSSION FOR SUCCESS IN MARRIAGE 111
   Marriage Identity 111
   Communication.. 118
   Balance Redefined 136
      Running a Business 142
      Having Children 144
      Educational Pursuits 148
      Marriage & Ministry 151
5 KEYS TO MAINTAINING A FRESH & THRIVING MARRIAGE 157
   Cultivating Environments 157
   Spontaneous Love 160
   Spending Quality Time Together with God 162
   Change of Scenery 165
   Revisiting Your Goal/Dreams 167
MIRROR MOMENTS 171

Conclusion 177

PRAYERS 179

Meet the Authors 183

DRS. MATTHEW & LATASHA NESBITT

INTRODUCTION

Solid relationships are about more than just having a companion. They are about more than romance. They are about more than the two people in them. Solid relationships are the foundation upon which solid communities are built; solid families build those communities. Maintaining a solid community impacts *everyone*. Even though many are successful in their marriages and relationships, they often don't have an opportunity to share keys to that success – keys which contribute to their communities. Consequently, we could not allow another year to pass, and could not pen another book without pausing to share some key elements of our collective success in relationships, marriage, and family. This project is a contribution from our family that we hope will impact generations to come.

We have been on our collective journey for just over a decade; during this brief time, we have learned and relied upon many valuable truths that have enhanced our lives, both individually and as a unit. There are countless books that cover dating and relationships, and myriad resources spanning topics regarding marriage and beyond. What makes our book unique is that it will provide you with a very candid opportunity to view the nuances of a relationship as it transforms and transports from singlehood to dating, through the engagement period, the beginning stages of marriage, and life beyond the wedding. Unlike most books, we share both a "his" and 'hers" perspective to allow you, the reader, to gather a sense of the often-perplexing dynamics of both sides of the relationship.

Relationships can be complex. Though only two people are involved, they bring with them their families, their various issues, perspectives, ideologies, and behaviors. These complexities cause many to continuously fail at love. We want to reveal to you some of our complex experiences, while providing hope beyond the broken places. That, along with some with practical tools, will enable you to go from one level of success to the next.

The key to successful relationships is mastering your current life stage. This mastery ultimately prepares you to unlock and advance in the next life's stage: once you have mastered being a single person, for example, only then can you properly transition and prepare for a healthy dating relationship. Many have skipped the primary stages and their relationships ultimately end in failure, but the fact is that these stages can be very difficult to navigate. Many times, we've skipped stages of mastery because we are conditioned to seeking that next relationship. However, with mastery of one stage, failure becomes evitable. However, failure is no longer an option for you!

We feel that transparency in sharing our experiences and providing some practical principles and tools will assist you in navigating this complex topic. In whatever stage you find yourself - single, dating, married, or even divorced - this book is designed to strengthen you right where you are. We witnessed God do a quick work in our relationship as He revealed Himself to be the Lord of our rings. We are ecstatic to share our journey with you. Buckle up!

Mirror Moments

At the conclusion of each chapter, there is a section called Mirror Moments. Mirror Moments are inclusive of five questions that are garnered from each chapter, in addition to four succeeding pages that are designed for note taking or jotting of concept or ideas. Mirror Moments are opportunities for you to reflect on YOU. They are designed to reveal the truth about who you are and how you can work to become better relationally. Apostle Paul speaks about how there are treasures in earthen vessels. There is a treasure inside of you that God designed for you to share with someone else. However, many times we are so focused on the other party in the relationship that we never focus on the value of what we bring to a relationship.

DRS. MATTHEW & LATASHA NESBITT

1

SINGLENESS

Hers

Daring to be Different

I was what many considered a late bloomer. While I didn't spend most of my childhood fantasizing about it, I somehow knew that I would one day have a family of my own. I was always involved in many extra-curricular activities, so getting into a relationship was not a forthright priority for me. I was enthralled with dancing and performing. From the time I was six years old, I would beg the cheer squad coach, Ms. Barron, to allow me to join the team. She would remind me that I was too young, but soon as the time allowed, I was there. As the youngest member of the team, I tried my best to keep up and flow with the big girls. I was a slow learner, but the thrill that came once I mastered a routine was almost surreal. My whole life was school, practice, eat, homework, and sleep for many years. My elementary and middle school years were about cheering or dancing. High school involved the same, to an even greater degree. I did well in school and was active in many other ways, too: I was a student council representative; I played clarinet in the marching band; I was captain of our dance team; I was a member of the school's law team for a short time; I was a member and then president of the National Honor Society; I was a member of the drama team. Because I was consistently busy, and my days and nights were not filled with boyfriend/girlfriend drama, it was what many would consider 'different.' It was certainly different from the typical drama-filled lifestyles that I witnessed some of my friends endure. It was different from the unexpected pregnancies that became so prevalent. Different from the curiosity of trying recreational drugs. Different from the intense social pressures of dying to be like everyone around me.

While things were different for me, I can remember a boy-friend or two; one played basketball alongside our cheer squad, another was a band member who played in the percussion section and had a little crush. I gave up a kiss or two, but nothing serious. I attended my senior prom with a classmate, the brother of a very good friend of mine. He came from a respectable family and I could trust him to drive me safely to and from the prom. Or so I thought. Well before iPods and Bluetooth capabilities, he had a cd mastered and strategically cued it to play "sex driven slow jams" on our way home. I guess it was supposed to get me in the what-goes-down-after-the-party mood. As our car proceeded down the pavement, I had to practically hang out the window to hide my laughter. It was laughable for me - laughable because while he and I had been in the band together and even attended a few National Honor Societies meetings together, we didn't have any kind of relationship that would suggest sex. I guess he hadn't got the memo about my indifference. While I had a shapely physique, I never gave the impression that prom night would be the night for "us." I don't think any physique or impression mattered though; for some it was the norm for high schoolers to engage in reckless sexual behavior. I was different, and it was okay.

Before prom, one of the guys who had shared lots of time with me in the drama club had begun to pursue me. He was an eloquent speaker and a highly charismatic personality. I allowed a bit of time for him. We traded gifts during birthdays, and I remember frequent letters and chocolate and stuffed teddy bears at Valentine's Day. We shared a kiss or two, but just before prom I learned he had stolen money from our locker and blatantly lied about it. His master manipulation was not attractive, and things didn't persist between us for long. We shared a few different activities because of school, and we maintained a friendship, but never entertained anything on a romantic level again. It was upsetting for my trust to be betrayed, but I went on with life.

My differences seem to work well for me. When I look back at my high school yearbook and browse the "class notables" section, I was voted most popular, best all around, and most school spirit. And though 20 years have passed since I walked those high school halls, when I talk to my former classmates, they tell me much of how I am today, is who I was back then. Though I didn't make time to find my high school sweetheart, high school represented some of the best times of my life. Through my involvement in various activities, I got to experience various cultural avenues and explore many of my passions.

If you are a high schooler, or anybody for that matter, and you are reading this book, I want you to know that it's okay for you to be you. I know, especially with the advent of peer pressure via social media, many will suggest that being different is wrong. I want you to know that it's okay. Being different is what can change the world. It's something I plan to do one day, and I pray you would too!

Lack of Identity & Vulnerability

Though difference is what defined me, I walked my high school halls with a lot of uncertainties. My Dad was married to a lady who was not my mom, but he still played an active role in my life. He did homework with me after school, took me shopping and purchased me anything I wanted, and was the most affectionate person I knew. However, during my junior year of high school he disappeared. Those afterschool visits suddenly ceased. Shopping days were cancelled, and the loving affection was a thing of what felt like a very distance past. What happened to my Daddy?

My freshman book project, *Unfinished Business,* explores in detail my journey to find out about my dad and his family, but there persisted in me a level of dissatisfaction regarding my family and my identity. There was this huge *something* missing that left with it a void and caused a great level of vulnerability. Knowing what I know now, this was an extremely dangerous place. While I didn't know how to effectively or adequately express what I was feeling, I felt cheated. I smiled often, yet I was angry. Angry that life dealt a blow that would render me fatherless. Angry that God had chosen me to bear such a burden. I had been a good Christian. I attended church, but more than that, I strived to live by its principles. I did right by people and was a "good" kid. What had I done to deserve this?

Bonded by Brokenness

Soon, it was time for college. I left home. I did well in class and the college adjustment period wasn't much of a strain. I learned independence. I explored various school organizations and joined a sorority during my second year of school. I had the opportunity to develop some lasting relationships, but still this void was present.

During the summer before my junior year of college, I entered a gravely dangerous relationship. It was riddled with control and manipulation, and sought to suffocate my identity. For the first time, I began to understand spirituality in an entirely different way. That relationship left with it a spirit of arrested development. Though the relationship seemed profitable, my personal growth was stunned. The lurking spirit in the relationship has a goal to identify a broken person and use their brokenness as a means to control their life and livelihood. During intense times of brokenness, or if there are unresolved issues that leave deep wounds, it is important to seek trusted sources. With great naivety, I had entered a relationship with another severely broken being. Brokenness plus brokenness only breeds more brokenness. ***I think the greatest tragedy, and the basis of all unhealthy relationships, is the subconscious thought, "this is the person who will heal me."*** In fact, neither are qualified to fill the other's emptiness. I believe this is the tragedy of some divorces, or even dating relationships - because we haven't taken time to heal, we ultimately spill our issues onto others, and remain unfulfilled in the area where healing is needed the most. This creates a regrettable cycles of unhappiness. You have committed to another, but seeking help and refuge from someone else who isn't equipped to handle the fullness of your pain can only lead to disaster.

Don't become bound by your broken. **Healing is your responsibility.** Take time to heal so you won't spill. When you don't take the time to heal sometimes you can find yourself in compromised relationships that are not in alignment with God's destiny for your life. Before it's realized, you've spent countless years in situations, in lifestyles, arrangements that are grossly beneath your designed purpose.

However, it is critical that you are cautious of which doors you allow to open especially because of lack of identity, or feelings of loneliness. One or two encounters while broken, with another broken person, can cost you time in a spiritual prison from which you could spend a lifetime attempting to break free.

Stop Looking & Start Living

As time went on, I joined a sorority and some of the frat guys would show interest. I entertained a few dates here and there, but nothing life altering. It was not until I was in my mid-twenties that I began to feel an internal pressure to make "something" happen relationally. By this time, I had become the quintessential bridesmaid in all my friends' weddings. There was the constant pressure of when I would get "booed up;" when was my mate going to arrive? It was a silent struggle. Like many of you, I subconsciously wondered if my time would ever come. Several times, I told myself, "It's getting late here, you better get moving." Somehow, I had developed a sense of what some would consider pride, while others might suggest it was faith. It was something down on the inside of me that earnestly believed that it would all work out just *when* it needed to. However, I began to develop my list. The infamous list that described that premade person who would complete me was up for review!

The List

You know, that list! You maybe didn't write yours down, but you know you have one! For us girls, I'm not sure where this list originates. Perhaps it's from various encounters of disappointment and self-protection: "I bet this won't happen again; my next is going to HAVE TO BE…" **Essentially, the faults of the EX contribute to the idealistic NEXT.** Perhaps it's this running list that has been tabulating since we first learned the notions of life, love, and happiness. Whatever it is…this list is there. And boy was mine ever-present! It went a little something like this:

1. He had to love God more than he loved me.
2. He had to be a virgin.
3. He needed to be politically conscious.
4. He had to be racially perceptive.
5. He had to be well-traveled.
6. He had to wear dreds or have a bit of length to his hair.
7. He had to have noticeable physical strength (buff).

8. No children preferably, but it was not totally a game changer.

You would think I would care if they had been divorced, or what kind of credit they had, or something more life-impacting. Ninety-nine percent of this stuff is laughable now! Anyway, this was the list of my non-negotiables. Subconsciously, whenever someone approached me and I sensed even in the slightest way that they violated one of my listed principles, I didn't really take the encounter seriously.

However, once I got to the point of believing it was time and feeling the pressure of getting on track to be married, I tested that list. Anytime I would learn of a virgin male, I'd test the waters. It was sort of bold, but silly. I know, it was bad! I remember sending an email to this one guy I knew (he was a minister and I'd learned of his virginity) about the possibility of him being my husband, only to later learn he was already engaged! I WAS A FIRST-CLASS FOOL!

I just knew I had a list and that list needed to be fulfilled and number 1 and number 2 were essential components of that list. Hence, man of God + virgin = mine, so I thought. Then, during a trip to visit family in Atlanta, I met another guy just as I was leaving church.

While exiting the sanctuary this guy stopped me. As the conversation ensued, I learned he was well-traveled and very politically astute. We wound up talking about politics and current events for nearly an hour. Maybe this could be him? We traded numbers. I traveled back to my home and he to his. We stayed in touch. We would spend hours on the phone discussing, debating, and sharing about all sorts of things. Things were going pretty well. We learned each other's schedules and soon become fixtures in each other's lives. Then, five months in, he shared that he had four children. We were five months in and never did he share (and neither did I ask) about children! My newness and naivety to the dating scene led me to believe that because he was spending so much time with me, neither wife, girlfriends, nor children were a part of his equation. I assumed he was truly "single." Not so. Though he claimed to be single, he had fathered four children in the United Kingdom. After hearing my shock, he began to use things that I had shared with him against me. He knew that I was a virgin and that I was approaching 25. He tried to sell me on the fact that our relationship could be the perfect scenario: since I was approaching the age for a high-risk pregnancy and didn't even know whether I could even *have* kids, his 4 would be perfect for me. Long story short, the conversations begin to dwindle. I shared with a friend his idea of my potential high-risk pregnancy and possible infertility, and she said, "You know what, he's probably right." I think she just wanted me to find SOMEBODY! She had gotten desperate for me, too! But I felt in my heart of hearts that something wasn't right. It was as if he had tried to invoke a sense of fear in order to get what he wanted. It nearly worked.

However, things begin to shift. As weeks passed, the conversations ceased between us. I cut it off officially in September of that year; I had finally come to my senses. I had gotten to the point of truly believing that if God had someone for me HE WOULD FIND ME! I don't know where I had developed a sense of needing to make it happen for myself. It was crazy that I felt a need to formulate a list and then go out as if I was perusing the grocery aisles and pick off the shelf the things that I believed were designed for me. I think in many relationships, this is one of the first places we feel out of control. Especially if you are a control freak like me, entering a relationship, or waiting to enter a relationship can be one of the most unnerving times because it is the place where you just have to wait. Especially for women, you don't know where is he is, where he's coming from, and when he's going to get there. But I learned quickly that life is about giving and selling out to God in a way that He knows He's priority and nothing and nobody else comes before Him. This is exactly what happened in my life.

Though I had been born and reared in the church, what I was pursuing was new. I laid down my list and began to seek out a life of connecting with God even more. I began to develop my prayer life. While I had been a practicing Christian my entire life, I took time to delve in and develop and get to know God at another level. I maximized my time with God. I fasted and prayed. I learned the art of intense prayer. None of my prayers were about getting into a relationship. As I begin to focus on God, my desires for a relationship were practically non-existent. I wanted to heal in ways that were critical for me. God begin to show me attitudes and ideologies that I had developed over time that were unlike Him. It was a time of intense spiritual recalibration. My relationship with God entered new realms.

I was in graduate school and I had a roommate. Any free time I had I would use to maximize the presence of God. I would really take time and get broken before God. I wanted to learn God's voice. I yearned to know Him in a real way. I wanted to know my purpose. I wanted to get back to the basics. This was a critical time for me. A time of connecting with family. Learning about identity. And healing from past wounds.

I wanted to know who I was and develop into the person God had called me to be, irrespective of anyone else. This was the most fulfilling time of my entire life. I'll chat about it a bit more during the next chapter, but the greatest practice I implemented then and still implement today is - instead of looking, searching, and seeking - taking inventory of my life.

Take Inventory

For many, singlehood can be a time of grave frustration. However, it can be used as a time for intensive inventory. As the owner of several businesses, I've learned that inventory, though time consuming, is a very necessary part of running a productive business. When you conduct an inventory, you consider what you have and what you still need. You consider the product that has been depleted, and what needs to be restocked. If you are anything like me, you despise going into an establishment and finding that they are "out of" something. I believe it's disrespectful to run out of products yet still advertise. **This is what we often do in relationships: we advertise things we really can't offer.** Inventory means a few things. Dictionary.com (2018) defines it as "a complete listing of merchandise or stock on hand, work in progress, **raw materials**, finished goods on hand, etc., made each year by a business concern." Raw materials are those materials that are there *before* being processed or manufactured. Why is this important? I'm so glad you were kind enough to ask. Have you taken inventory of your raw materials? What materials do you have that are useable in a relationship? They might not be fine-tuned yet, but during singleness, take inventory of some of what *you* have to offer. Ask yourself and explore some very significant questions:

- Do I know how to properly love someone?
- How and where did I learn how to love?
- When did I learn what it means to be a good friend?
- How do you become a "good" person? What kind of qualities do friends possess?

I explored these sorts of questions and many of my answers were derived from what I learned or had adopted through previous relational experiences. Admittedly, I can't recall conversations where either of my parents or grandparents sat me down and said, "this is how you know you love someone," or, "this is what makes you a good friend." When I answered these questions for myself, I discovered that many of the relationship behaviors and philosophies that I had adopted as "healthy" were altogether flawed. Taking inventory is critical because of the brokenness that comes from many of our past relationships. *We spend lots of time in our singleness attempting to recreate what love is because we have learned for sure what love isn't. Because we know what love isn't, we somehow think we are equipped with the necessary skills to build adequate relationships.* But if I have a flat tire on my car, having the tools to fix it doesn't mean I know HOW to fix it. A spare and a jack are useless to me unless I have developed the adequate skills to utilize them. While I may have the tools, there are essential skills I need to learn and practice in order to evolve theoretical knowledge into practical wisdom.

Singleness is a time to establish what adequately loving yourself means, and how can you translate that love to another person. How flexible are you in learning this? Don't rush singleness, instead allow it to be a discovery stage that develops you into the ideal mate.

Don't waste your singleness. Take time to conduct an inventory. Not that this inventory is the fullness of who you are, but it is the beginning steps of actively and consciously considering how valuable you can be in a relationship.

When I am unfulfilled in relationships, even friendships, I move from complaining to becoming the person I wish I had. Taking inventory allows you to analyze the surplus as well as the deficits. Once these assessments are made, the areas of deficit can become places on which to focus for improvement. This is where real growth and self-improvement happens. These small changes can transform the essence of who you are and who you hope to become.

SINGLENESS

His

I've always been a relationship kind of guy. My first crush was in first grade, and by second grade I'd progressed to writing the "do you like me, circle yes or no" love letters. Even on through middle school and high school, I was pretty much always found in some type of relationship with one young lady or another. None of them were extremely serious or lasted beyond a year. I just enjoyed the notion of being in a relationship and having someone around at all times. And although I enjoyed those short-term relationships, I always knew that I wanted something more permanent – I wanted to be married and have children. I really wanted to "dime up" a wife and be a family man. In my dreams (and on paper), I had everything laid out. One day it would be picture perfect: a house, a white picket fence, and cute kids.

Right after college, however, I was confronted with some major realities. My life hit a brick wall. I was about 22, and I was getting older and becoming frustrated with myself. I wasn't this starry-eyed teenager anymore. The things that I was accustomed to doing in my relationships were no longer working for me. There was no sense of fulfillment. My relationships weren't growing properly and definitely headed in the wrong direction. I finally had to come to grips with some of my ideologies, and I began unfolding some dysfunctional patterns and behaviors in my relationships. I discovered that there were areas of my life that needed some major work. In order to prepare myself for what I envisioned long-term, I had to finally embrace this whole idea called "singleness." This would prove to be a challenging but necessary endeavor.

By the time I was 23 years old, and I was entertaining a few relationships and talking to multiple young women at the same time. This kind of juggling act was very familiar to me; it was my comfort zone. But I knew it was time to do something different. I kept all my phone numbers in my infamous "black book." Actually, I was evolving, and had also started storing them in my Blackberry phone. I know, I know; I'm showing my age here.

Anyway, one afternoon I sat on my bed and did a major sweep. I started erasing numbers out of my phone, and I threw my black book away…yes, you heard me…I tossed it! I had made up in my mind that I needed some time to myself, and I refused to entertain any more relationships. I knew these women would wonder what happened that made me stop calling, but I chose not to do a whole lot of explaining. I just came up missing. I stopped taking calls that I usually answered, and I stopped reaching out to others all together. I know you might be thinking that this was drastic, but it was necessary. I realized that my unaddressed dysfunction was not only affecting my own growth and development, but it was also causing harm to those I was in relationship with. I could no longer function in relationships without doing it properly; I had to get myself together.

I want to do lay out a few points below that were crucial in my singleness:

Scattered Pieces

When I started to examine most of my relationships, I began to find some consistent patterns. In most of my relationships, the woman always served as a piece to an incomplete puzzle; she fulfilled only a small segment of my desire. So, I found myself not settled and always feeling the need to have multiple types of female relationships in my life. Let me explain: I would have one woman that I could merely talk to and just engage in good conversation; I'd have another who was cool enough to hang out with my guys and have fun; another who was just head over heels in love and would do anything for me; and yet another for physical attractiveness and fun in the bedroom. I know it seems like a lot, but this is the reality for a lot of guys. So, I found myself juggling - investing energy into those who could fill the void at that given time. I wouldn't say that I had any evil intentions or horrible motives; in fact, I really prided myself on being honest, sincere, and true to any relationship. But my thinking was warped; I wasn't whole within myself and started grabbing for pieces to fill the empty spots. ***In my time of singleness, I discovered that possessing scattered pieces never provides true***

wholeness.

Relationships present one of the few cases where mathematically, the numbers just don't add up. It would seem that more relationships would lead to greater value. But this is not true! In relationships, we sometimes believe that the more people we can call boyfriend/girlfriend/friend, the happier we are. Because each scattered piece serves a need, you might be under the impression that you are being fulfilled. You could be reading this book and think you have a lot of "potentials" in your life, but at the end of the night you come home lonely, to the reality of an unfulfilled life. All of those relationships you have going are not fulfilling and you still feel alone. Those relationships might serve as temporary fixes or things to keep you occupied, but don't provide long-lasting peace. And out of convenience, we can find ourselves holding on to these random pieces, thinking somehow it will equate to wholeness. That's not how it works! It's only when you clear the cluttered space in your life that you allow yourself to detox, eliminating the clutter. ***I wanted to be prepared for what was coming and had to learn that less will ultimately lead to more.***

In order to gain better clarity and align my life to my future, I decided to do 40 days of prayer, fasting, and soul searching. Yeah, 40 days! I highly recommend this in preparing yourself for future relationships. I had undergone times of fasting before with my previous church, but never in my life had I felt such a push to really self-discover and allow God to further develop me in my time of singleness. This was a totally new space in my life. But I had to set boundaries and establish time for true singleness. It's difficult. No, let me say it another way: It was **VERY** difficult!

You might be reading this section at a time when it seems like you are all alone in the world. That means that you are in one of the most powerful positions that you can be in. There are some things that can only be learned when you dedicate time by yourself, alone and single. God will strip you of all of the 'fluff' in your life to get you down to the lowest common denominator: YOU! If these relationships remain in your life as mere fragments you will never unlock true wholeness. God will remove all of these crutches only to give you the maturity and strength needed to stand on your own…and eventually stand united with someone else. Singleness really takes the focus off other people and causes us to shine the light on ourselves. Many people don't like this stage. It's tough. It's real. It's candid. During singleness you can finally come to grips with the reality of who you really are and discover what's needed to gain wholeness within yourself.

My time of soul-searching and singleness revealed 5 major areas to improve:

1.   Understanding History

My singleness caused me to start asking the question, "WHY?" I wanted to understand my behaviors and some of the patterns that I was trapped in. I was tired of seeing the manifestations on the tree, but never getting to the root of the issue. I sought to get to the source of my dysfunctions instead of merely changing my behaviors. A great starting place for me was taking time to reflect on my history and some of the events that had transpired in my life. I knew that it was impossible for me to embrace my future, unless I got a handle on my past. Some of you are trying to move forward without ever confronting where you've been. You must ask questions like: What are some of the things that shaped my perspectives in relationships? When did I notice a change in my behavior? What unresolved issues from my past are hindering my future? When I started asking myself these questions, God began revealing the answers.

I was blessed with two amazing parents. They were married through my early teen years, and my two older brothers and I were raised in a two-parent household. They divorced when I was around 12, after 20 years of marriage. I would say that I took it rather well. Both of my parents handled things with great maturity; they kept us as the focal point and maintained a loving and supportive atmosphere in both of their respective homes. Although I coped well outwardly, I subconsciously developed some behaviors that I had to revisit during my singleness. Of which, I will discuss in detail below.

2. Delayed Closures

I started to discover that I could easily start a relationship with someone, but it was very difficult for me to bring closure to it. I would keep a relationship going even if I thought it wasn't headed in the right direction... or headed nowhere at all. I would find myself still talking with the person, stringing them along, and trying to avoid totally removing them from certain space in my life. So, I found myself maintaining a bunch of relationships that ended up being headaches and weights, because I simply didn't effectively communicate their placement in my life. Closure was a major problem. All these 'pieces' of relationships were adding up and causing me extra stress and no real happiness. They weren't what I needed. They weren't what I wanted. They didn't even reflect where I was going. We often refuse to close the door of past relationships, which prevents an open door to the future.

Like me, some of you have some relationships that you need to bring closure to. **In relationships, there are necessary endings that lead to the path of newly found beginnings**. Could it be that the relationships you refuse to release are sources of clutter, blocking the arrival of the next? You will never know until you have the power to simply let go. Don't get me wrong, there are some things worth fighting for. But, most of what we are fighting for are temporary fixes and not eternal connections. I had to discover the difference. Temporary fixes won't last; they accommodate where you are but don't reflect where you are going. Although they can cause instant pleasure, they can also cause long-term pain. What I needed in my life wasn't a temporary fix. I was seeking a life-long relationship that reflected my future. I had to end the cycle. I wasn't going to spend another 10 years going in circles, making no real progress. Letting go and ending some relationships was the first step in the right direction.

3.   Fear of Being Alone

I reflected on my parent's relationship and decided that I never wanted to be alone. Seeing their divorce gave me the drive and desire to have a long-lasting relationship. I didn't want my relationships to come to an end; deep down ending any relationship reminded me of the divorce. Although this could be viewed as a great aspiration, it caused to me to lower my standards in relationships. I just felt the need to always be with someone. I felt that I always needed someone I could vibe with and talk to. I thought I always had to have at least one option. At the end of the day, I didn't want to be caught doing this thing called "life," alone. And that is a major truth for many of you who are single. You have a fear of being alone. You entertain the questions: What if there is no one out there for me? What if I end up single for a long, long time? What if I can't ever find the right match? Instead of waiting and developing yourself, you jump in and out of relationships and find yourself searching, but at the same time settling. You end up settling for someone who doesn't meet your standards. Most of us started out with a laundry list of things a potential mate needed to bring to the table before we would even look their way! But soon you find yourself compromising and accepting almost anything. You find yourself settling for someone who is not fully invested in the relationship like you are, or settling for someone who treats you as an option and not a king or queen. You find yourself at the point of desperation only so that you don't end up alone.

Let's put this thing in perspective. What's the big rush? To whom or what are you comparing your life? Who said you needed to be married by a certain age? Who said that you needed to have children by any given date? This is all self-inflicted pressure that you have placed upon yourself. Slow down! Take your time! Relax! ***You have to cancel out all of that fear and come to acknowledge that it's better to be alone than in an unhealthy relationship***. I ultimately had to come to grips and break the illusion that being alone meant having a horrible life. That wasn't the reality. That wasn't what God had planned for me. I could no longer live in that space of fear and be bound by its ability to keep me stuck and immobilized. When I started releasing the pressure, my purpose began to surface.

4. Soul Ties

During my time of consecration and soul-searching, I came to a better understanding something called soul-ties. By spending time, sharing your heart and energies, and having intimate exchanges with someone, you start to intertwine your soul with that individual. The word "soul" literally means your mind, will, and emotions. That's why some people say that they are single, but find their souls still united with the person they claimed to have left. So, it's possible to break-up with someone, and not be in their physical space or even in the same city, but still be tied to them. Now that's deep!

Singleness was necessary for me because it gave me the time to acknowledge and break unhealthy soul ties. It had become so easy for my thoughts to be attached to some of the people I'd been in relationships with. Many of you don't think outside the boundaries of your relationship with a person, and you find that all of your thoughts are wrapped around them - whether you should go certain places, do certain things, or make certain decisions for your life and future. Instead of making your own decisions from a place of freedom, you allow them to keep influencing everything.

Soul ties can affect your will and emotions. You feel indifferent about things that you once loved and were passionate about. Goals that you established for yourself and the steps needed to achieve them are now growing dim because your primary focus is the relationship. You find that your emotions are all out of control. If they are mad, you get mad. If they aren't interested, you decide you aren't interested either! You no longer have much control over your own emotions. Your emotions become fickle; one conversation can alter your whole mood for the day. One disappointment can move you from a state of complete joy to a day filled with gloom and frustration. Through all of it, you are losing the essence of who you are. Singleness is essential for your own sanity. Remember, true and healthy relationships are not designed for you to lose yourself in the process.

True singleness is a process of letting go of the past and removing yourself from unhealthy soul-ties. I had to detox and let go of past failures and emotional and physical connections, and gain the ability to think and act on my own volition. It's nearly impossible to enter into a relationship when we are unhealed. Those negative behaviors and cycles will manifest again in new relationships, ruining what was meant to bless you. I couldn't allow this in my life and knew that it was time to start this process so that I could be ready for the wife that was coming.

5. Necessary Deposits

Not only did I have to extract unhealthy thought processes and attachments from my life, but I also had to make some deposits. I often hear of people who go through the stage of singleness where they are doing some soul searching or have disconnected from some relationships. They might not have found Mr. or Ms. Right and are just waiting. And that sounds good, and to some it sounds cute! But it's not enough! What are you doing during this time of singleness? How are you using your time? I found out that I couldn't just isolate myself for the sake of isolation. I couldn't just be single and treat it as merely another stage in my life. **Your time of singleness is significant!** I had to be detoxed from the old and make new, substantial deposits in my life; I had to embrace wholeness. This moves you from the place of single and sobbing! Your singleness should not be a time where you are isolated and becoming more miserable. It's at this time that you can become depressed, unmotivated, discouraged, and have a negative outlook on relationships and your life as whole. *Singleness has nothing to do with your space but your ability to replace.* Let me explain.

I started to identify the areas of my life that I was filling up with relationships. These were areas of need in my life, places that were unhealed, underdeveloped, or simply void. And now that the people were removed, I had to replace them with principles and with my own passion. For example, I noticed I was spending a lot of my time and energies texting and talking on the phone. Of course, changing this was quite an adjustment. It had become a major part of my day. It was taking up lots of time - countless hours and minutes of my life. A light bulb went off and I started to see the valuable time I was wasting. Not only that, but I was neglecting my inner passion. I realized that I had given up on going back to graduate school and was settling on working a job because of a failed attempt in that area. I'd gotten off track. Two years had gone by and finally I was rediscovering my passion again. I had to learn myself all over again. You have to ask yourself these questions during your time of singleness: What do I actually like to do alone? What things provide me with happiness outside of other people? I started to focus on what God had called me to do and began strengthening areas that I was neglecting. It's very possible to get so wrapped up with other people, that you lose track of who you are.

I wanted God to take everything out of me that wasn't like Him. Take out lust and give me real love. Take out hurt and replace it with healing. Remove distraction and give me discipline. Remove the pushiness and give me patience. Take out selfishness and give me the heart of selflessness. *I didn't want to be anyone else's "man" until I was God's man.* I wanted to have character and integrity, and I soon learned that it needed the necessary time to be developed. I started investing in myself like crazy. Singleness was a great time of rediscovery and preparation for my next.

Mirror Moments

Questions

1. What are some "necessary endings" that are crucial for you to fully embrace your singleness?

2. Identify historical issues that could potentially hinder your future relationships.

3. List individuals with whom you have unhealthy soul ties?

4. Identify areas in which you are still broken.

5. What are some goals you are focused on (besides finding a mate) during your singleness?

Mirror Moments
Reflections

Mirror Moments

Reflections

Mirror Moments

Reflections

Mirror Moments

Reflections

DRS. MATTHEW & LATASHA NESBITT

2

DATING

Hers

After about six to eight months of intensive personal development, my friend Renisha invited me to an event celebrating a new ministry that had come to our college town. She had originally invited me to an event on a Friday, but because I was under the weather, so I declined that invitation. The following Saturday, I was headed to a different event across town, but once I arrived at my destination, the doors were locked. I later learned the event had at the same time taken place in the next town over. It seemed to be a case of right time, wrong place.

Determined to not make a waste of my trek across town using public transportation, I called Renisha and gave her an update.

She was excited to learn that I was only steps away from the weekend of events she had invited me to attend. She drove to pick me up. I didn't know the fullness of what was about to transpire, but as I got into her car and buckled the seatbelt I proclaimed, "Look at the Tasha you know now, because I won't be any longer. My life is about to change forever!" I didn't know the power of what I was saying, but I strongly believed that unbeknownst to me, my destiny had ensured that I was going to attend that event.

The event was a worship service geared towards training and equipping. After it was over, I left wanting to know more. I soon discovered that the people who were facilitating the event were starting a new ministry in the area. So, the following day, after I finished duties at my church, I rode with Renisha to the service for this new ministry.

The service was filled with joy and excitement, something I hadn't experienced at other churches in my college town. It was quite refreshing to witness. We stayed until the end of the service, and because we were new faces, a few people came and welcomed us. One guy came and spoke to my friend Renisha and me, and he also gave hugs. In fact, many people were being greeted in this way. This guy though, didn't give me the typical 2-3 second "church hug;" his was more like a 5-7 second one. He welcomed us to the church and entertained a substantive yet brief conversation. A few days later, Renisha came home all excited. I couldn't imagine what the fuss was about. "Tashi[1], I have great news! Guess who likes you?!" The elongated church hug crossed my mind. But before I had an opportunity to answer, she exclaimed, "Brother Matthew! He wants to take you out to eat!" I immediately retorted, "He could stand to lose about 15 pounds, but he's okay. And plus, nothing's wrong with a free dinner. Nothing." When I saw him again, he asked me to dinner. I agreed and picked the spot. We went to what was considered the most upscale place I knew at the time, a place called *Silvercreek*. I remember we had a great time. He picked me up from my place and we headed over. The conversation at dinner was great. I asked him what he thought his life's purpose was, and what were some things he wanted out of life. While I can't recall his exact statements, they were good enough to entertain the possibility of another date.

On the next date we went to eat and then to see a movie. It seemed swift, but our conversation was pretty serious from jump. I think it was during this second date that he revealed that he believed I was his wife. HOLD ON BROTHER! HOLD ON! He was pretty confident, and though he was a nice, charismatic guy, I had only come for the food. I had given up on matchmaking. I had recalibrated and was just flowing with life. Nothing serious involving anyone else, just flowing.

However, I saw that Matthew was serious in his efforts with

---

[1] Tashi was a nick name she called me.

me. We spent endless hours on the phone talking about our individual hopes and dreams. This was new, and it was amazing. A lot of our desires meshed. After a few months, our excitement had not diminished and finally I began to realize that maybe this was God. It was the first time that I hadn't tried to force something, and instead he had taken the lead. I began to seek God for signs. During my prayer time I asked the question forthrightly: Is Matthew (my husband)? Months passed, and one day while driving, God beckoned me to pull my car over on the side of the road. He spoke clearly and directed me to look over to my far right. There was a sign that read "700 N Mattis Ave." I looked quickly as there would soon be oncoming traffic. I took note and traveled along down the road. During my singleness, God had fine-tuned his voice and revealed witty ways that He communicated to me. He typically would give me signs and numbers that would have in-depth meaning. As I drove along, I burst into intense laughter. The sign and the numbered street had been an answered prayer. Biblically, seven is a number representing completion. And the street name is MATTIS(MATT-IS). I had asked God: Is Matthew? And there was the answer, specifically. Matthew would become the one I would eventually marry.

Though I hadn't spent many years on finding the right one, being found by Matthew was a relief. Dating was new for me. As girls, I think from a young age we subconsciously envision a life that consists of a family with a husband and wife, and a kid or two. To have met Matthew, and to understand that God had designed and fashioned someone to be able to handle the fullness of who I was - all the hurts, insecurities, all my hopes, my dreams, my fears, my faults, my strengths, my idiosyncrasies - provided me with a great level of peace. I was excited!

Though dating was a very brief phase in our relationship, I learned a lot about me, him, and us. We began to adjust our lives. We spent nearly every day together, and our lives began to intertwine in a marvelous way. Our friendships were tested, our faith was tried, but we trudged along the path of discovering one another. Along that path I learned some valuable lessons. Some of which, I will share below.

Sneak Peak

First, dating provides a preview of your mate's reality. I remember early on, perhaps starting with the third or fourth date, he would show up later than planned. Sometimes, once he made it to my place we would sit up front and watch a movie. A few times, ten minutes into the film, Matthew would be found snoring. At first, I fumed when this happened. My anger didn't last though, because it was funny how my #1 list requirement (him loving God) had become my nemesis.

It was difficult finally committing to someone only to learn that he had a greater commitment, and it was to God and physically building a new church. I had come to connect to my future, but had to share him in a very real way. Our relationship persisted, and the more we grew the more involved he became in ministry. Many times, we believe we can change a person, good or bad. However, what you see during the dating phase of a relationship is often what you get. Hence, I had to make peace with the fact that I was dating and would ultimately marry a PREACHER!

If you are dating, do you understand who you are dating? Are your futures compatible? Are you willing to sacrifice? Will you risk your happiness? The truth you see now will be the truth you will witness later. Prepare for it.

Growing up in church, and fine tuning my relationship with God, I knew there was a place in ministry as well. Hence, though I originally saw Matthew's entrenched involvement in church as an inconvenience to our budding relationship, it ultimately matched well with some of my own purposes in God.

Be Specific with God

Another key lesson worth sharing is the power of being specific with God. While some may laugh at the "sign" I received, it was a direct response to a very specific prayer. And while I didn't use it as my only indicator, it was a significant clue, one that allowed me to know that entering to a relationship of this magnitude was not something that I had spearheaded, but there were signs of God through it all. From my outrageous list of requirements, God granted me the *one* that has made the most impact on my life. The fact that I wanted a man that loved God more than He loved me let me know that no matter what we experienced, his desire to please God would outweigh any other issue. It meant that he would do right by me, because his primary goal was to please God. The bible speaks about how "life and death are found in the power of the tongue." Well before I knew who Matthew was, or that he even existed, I began to ask God about this. Just as I prayed for my son's wife and my daughter's husband before they were born, this specificity speaks about your level of expectancy. Be specific and watch God manifest what you TRULY need!

Make Time to Live Alone

Though I understood that there was a great possibility of a future between my soon-to-be fiancé and me, I had an opportunity to live by myself. Though it was only for about three months, taking the time to critically assess who I was, what I wanted to become, what I could give, how my presence contributed the world, and how it contributed to a relationship, built a foundation that was critical for a healthy relationship. I grew up with five other siblings. After leaving home, I went to a college dormitory setting. I had a roommate my freshmen and sophomore years of school, and my junior and senior years I lived a sorority house. While that marked the first time I had my own room, I had six to seven other housemates. Then in graduate school I had one roommate. Just before Matthew and I were getting married, there was a brief period where I lived alone. We, Matthew and I, signed a lease to the place we would ultimately stay together. I lived there for 4 months alone before we were married and Matthew moved in on our wedding. While I didn't originally plan it, this alone time was a necessary element in my development. It helped me to understand my own identity. Before merging as one, it's important to know what you like. In order to be happy in marriage, you must have a sense of fulfillment within yourself. It's imperative to learn to value your own presence. Listen to yourself think without the music playing. Listen to you without scrolling through social media. Do it without any background noise. Do it without the kids being there; do it before they get up for the day. *I believe this period of being alone will help you value YOU, and it will set the stage to give others permission to value you as well.*

There is much research that cites the number one reason for divorce as financial issues. Not to minimize that impact of finances on a household, but I will endeavor to say that the greatest reason for separation is a lack of personal fulfillment. Many seek marriage or other relationships because they are missing something only God can provide. Once they are married they soon learn that what they truly need does not reside in their mate Hence, I believe spending *necessary, intentional time alone* now can save you from a nasty separation later.

Assess What You Bring to the Table

Isolation can be painful, but many times is necessary. Assessing what you bring to the table is a solid and sure way to help each party understand their identity in marriage.

Marriage merges much, but it is essential for each partner to have a good sense of personal fulfillment as an individual. The time God allowed me before meeting Matthew was essential to my development as a woman and eventually a wife and a mother. I know many of you are saying, "Well I've been alone most of my life and now it's my time to be found by someone." And while that may very well be the case, I want you to assess whether your time "alone" is truly and intentionally geared towards self-development. I ask, because **wives are not made overnight (neither are husbands)!**

What are you doing now that will be beneficial to your future mate? What are you committed to that will change his life? What are you investing in that will propel him to a place of ultimate happiness? What are you doing now that will make him want to come home? What are doing now that will make him envision himself with you? The ultimate goal of any married person is to please the **other** person. It is truly about each party seeking solely to please the other. That might sound foreign, but most of the pleasing doesn't just happen in the bedroom, or even at the shopping mall. The question every married person should ask themselves is, "What can I give to the other person?"

I'm certain that you have heard the phrase several times before, but there is no handbook to marriage. Many of us learn how to be friends by the way friends have treated us or by the way we saw it done. The same goes for marriage: many of us have not witnessed examples of what it means to have a healthy marriage. We really don't know what we are doing when we leave the stage of singleness. This stage of *necessary, intentional time alone* becomes even more critical in understanding what it means to be a wife or husband. During this time, God can begin to download what it means to be a partner in marriage. You'll find yourself learning things and considering options that you hadn't before. In all, this *necessary, intentional time alone* is critical to understanding who you are and who you need to become.

True happiness in marriage is found when you understand how your value ultimately contributes to another's. I know that was heavy. But it is significant to consider this sole question in your singleness: What will somebody gain by adding **YOU** to their life?

I knew I was a worshipper. I knew I was passionate. I knew I was compassionate. I knew I was a God-lover. I knew I was an unjealous supporter. Most of this I knew before I met my husband. *So, when Matthew came along, I had to consider, how could my life fit his life without blending so much that I became invisible.* Some of us stop our lives and do only what our husbands or mates do, so after some time we become unfulfilled. While some of our desires should eventually be shared, all of them don't have to be. I see this a lot in ministry: wives or first ladies are there to support their husbands, but many have given up their individual lives. They walk around bitter about what they sacrificed for ministry, for the kids, taking care of elderly parents; they never got an opportunity to pursue their passions. While life is full of responsibilities, you must make space to discover the essence of why you were created. There is something specific that God called you to do that has nothing to do with your prospective mate, children, boss, or anyone else. Be sure to take some time to get to know these indispensable facts about you; it will ultimately enhance your union.

DATING

His

My time of singleness, which lasted just over one year, proved to be such a rewarding time. I embraced this time as an opportunity to allow God to heal me from my past, to rediscover myself, and to ready myself for all that was ahead. Although I knew singleness wasn't going to be my ultimate fate, I knew it was a necessary stage essential in the preparation for my future. I felt empowered, strengthened, restored, and refreshed with an entirely new God-given perspective. I could actually say that I felt ready to pursue a new relationship. This time I wasn't looking for a short-term fling just to keep me occupied. I wasn't looking for someone who could merely fulfill one part of my life. I wanted a complete woman! I wanted someone who could handle the totality of who I was and one I could spend the rest of my life with. I wasn't looking for someone just to date, but I wanted a woman I could date with the clear intention to marry. I had read Proverbs 18:22 for many years, and I wanted to find my "good thing." I was excited. I was hopeful. I was ready!

How we met

At the time, I was really focused on music and playing for my church. Our ministry was a start-up and fairly new to the community where we lived. We were holding services in a temporary location, and we were seeing lots of new faces. Word was getting around about the ministry and we had frequent guests. Some of those guests were residents from the community, but many were attending the University as undergraduates or graduate students. As a keyboardist, I had the best view! I could see everyone who was coming in and out of the services, and I didn't miss a beat. I had the best seat in the house. I will never forget the Sunday one of our members, Renisha, brought a friend with her to visit. I saw them as they walked in and kind of kept an eye on them throughout the worship service. After service, I got off the keyboard and started to greet everyone, as I normally did. I then made my way to the back of the church and bumped into Renisha and her friend. I hugged Renisha and then introduced myself to her friend. And instead of shaking her hand, I reached out and gave her a hug. Now, you have to understand me. My family and I are very affectionate people. Many people say that my brothers and I give some of the best hugs! So, I was thinking in my mind, "Let me give her one of those good ol' Nesbitt hugs!" She smiled but didn't seem fazed one bit.

I didn't know what I was feeling, but there was something different and something special about her. She caught my eye. She had my attention. And, it was kind of weird because it was deeper than, "Man, she is so fine, and I want her." Although she was very easy on the eye, that was not even the space I was in. I had changed, and I wasn't on that level anymore. I saw something deeper, but I just couldn't make sense of it. It felt good. It was different. It was new! It was such a great feeling that I was caught up in the moment and…I forgot her name!

The next Sunday, she came to service again! The moment she came through the door, it's like everything about her lit up. I don't know if she put a little extra time into getting dressed or whatever, but she definitely walked in with a presence. She had my attention. I stayed focused during service and wasn't going to allow my attention to be moved away from God, but I sure wasn't letting her leave without talking to her! I think she might have gotten up to use the restroom or get a drink, and I was counting down the time for her to get back. Where did she go? She coming back? She good? What she doing?! When service let out I wanted to make sure to speak with Renisha and her friend. They got separated and it gave me a chance to talk to Renisha alone for a brief second. And I started asking as many questions as possible: What's your friend's name? Is she a student? How old is she? She got a dude? And the only question she had time to answer was her name. She responded, "Her name is Tasha." She then asked me, "Why you asking?!" I smiled, and she smiled and said, "Oh, somebody like somebody huh?!" Like I was in fifth grade or something. I told her to stop playing and go ahead and put in the word for me. And she did.

Not a week later, Tasha ended up joining the church! We had a major conference the week after, and I got a chance to speak with her more extensively. And the more I engaged her in small talk, the more confident I was that my feeling was right. She wasn't your typical female. There was something very special about her. I wanted to talk more. I wanted to discover who she really was. By this time, I'm sure that she had talked with Renisha. And I later found out that, unbeknownst to me, my dad also came up to her and told her about me. I had never even told my dad anything about her or that I was interested! Anyway, she had my total attention and I didn't want to let things go any further without her hearing it directly from me. I still didn't know anything about her except she was attending the University and was in graduate school. Was she dating someone else? Was she interested in me? Did I catch her eye? At this point, I didn't even care about the answer to any of those questions! An entire month had gone by and I surely wasn't going to waste any more time wondering. I needed her number; I was going to check out the scene for myself!

Our first date

We exchanged numbers and started conversing outside of church. The vibe was cool, but I still didn't know much about her. The time at church was too limited and texting and talking on the phone wasn't doing it for me. I wanted to see her face to face! I was just going to go out on a limb and ask her if I could take her out to dinner. So, one day I told her that I wanted to take her out and just talk. I'll never forget her response. She said, "Yes, but what do you want with me?" I was taken aback because I didn't expect for her to be so forthcoming. I explained that I wasn't one to play a lot of games, and I really wanted to get to know her. I told her that we would sit down and just chat and get to know each other, and wherever things went, they went. I could tell she was a little apprehensive but was definitely open to finding out who I was and what I was all about. I am not going to lie: I was super hyped!! We would finally get the chance to sit down and go out on a real date. I told her that I had a few places in mind that where we could eat, but I was open for her to choose the place. She decided on a low-key, sleeper spot called *Silvercreek*. That by itself spoke volumes. She didn't say Red Lobster or Olive Garden. Although those are good places, they are typical and expected. Wow!

I remember getting ready for the date. I wanted to make sure that I had a fresh cut, solid outfit, smelled good, and that my car was super clean when picking her up! At that time, I drove a mint green 1996 Ford Explorer. I took it to the carwash and vacuumed it out really good and had it fresh and smelling good. I had also recently got flat-screen tv's installed for the front and back seats. I had speakers in the back, and I selected some nice chill music to listen to as well. When I arrived at her complex, I just knew she had nice taste. I had driven by this place multiple times, but never knew anyone that stayed there. I came to the entrance and was met at the gate by a guard. I told them here name and gave them her apartment number. They called her and got approval and sent me around to the right of the complex, almost at the very back. I texted her and told her that I was downstairs. I will never forget: she came down the steps with a bright yellow blouse and jade green skirt with some sandals. I opened the door for her and let her in the truck. She looked around the truck like she was taking note of things and checking everything out.

We had an amazing time at dinner. The conversation just flowed; the vibe was super cool with no dead spots or uncomfortable moments. It felt really good! We got a chance to learn a little bit about each other and the space we were at in our lives. She discovered more about me being from the area and attending the University. She learned about my role at the church and my heart for ministry. She told me about growing up in Chicago and how she was finishing her Master's degree, that she was attending another church, and how God led her to the ministry I attended. She was really on a quest for a deeper experience with God. It was a night I will never forget. But the question came up again, "What do you want with me?" And on our very first date, not having spent much time with her, not knowing all of the ins and outs of who she was, I responded and told her that I wanted to pursue a relationship with her, not just to date for a long time and play around, but with the intent to marry. I told her, "I believe you are my wife!" I know it sounds crazy, but I did! With everything that was on the inside of me, I believed that she not only was someone I would date, but someone I wanted to marry. She literally laughed and me and said, "You really believe that, huh?!" But at no point did she negate it or reject it. And that gave me so much peace. In that short time, I knew she wasn't a woman for a lot of big talk and lip service. I saw her listening and would allow the days ahead to determine if what I saw would become a reality.

That night was the beginning of something great for us! Although we would have many experiences that forged our relationship, this night was the first official night we started dating. Little did I know that God was doing a quick work with us. During this process of dating, I learned some very valuable lessons and practical principles that are worth sharing. These are the things that worked for us and that I believe will bless you!

Before you go Public

We were both extremely excited that we were now officially dating! It was fresh, it was new, and it was a major stage of our lives. We had found love and couldn't wait to see where the relationship would take us. Of course, we wanted everyone to know. We both had numerous relationship circles: family, friends, church, school, sorority members, etc. We wanted them to be able to share in our happiness and celebrate this new, exciting stage that we had entered. One of the most valuable lessons that I learned when dating was **don't go public until you have mastered the private.**

Some people just can't wait to go public! You've got it all in your head about how you are going to post about it on Facebook or Instagram. You've even got the picture you are going to use, where you both are hugged up and looking cute! We all naturally want that support. The likes, the hearts, the "ya'll cute," and "I'm happy for ya'll!" We want to get the word out there and let everyone see the happiness that we are experiencing. And I don't believe there is anything wrong with that desire, but I do believe that some of you do it prematurely. I want to share with you what worked for Tasha and me.

We treated the beginning stages of our dating like a newborn baby! Your baby (relationship) must grow and mature properly in the early stages to have a long, successful life span. Early in our dating I learned two important keys:

1. Building Immunity

Newborn babies are in their most vulnerable stage. Parents must take special measures to ensure that the growth process is not compromised. Now I know it's old school, but you don't come out with a baby in public until after six to eight weeks. LOL! I see some people coming out two days later with the baby dressed in a onesie and some Jordans! I don't care how excited and thrilled you are about your baby, studies show that your baby is unable to handle various external elements until his or her immune system is strengthened. The same is true in a relationship; you can't start dating someone one week and expose your vulnerabilities in the community, at church, or on social media the next. Your relationship needs time to develop its immunity. Many of our relationships are publicized prematurely. The picture looks cute, your smiles look fresh, but you have to know that everyday isn't pretty! You haven't even had your first argument! You haven't successfully navigated a relationship breakdown. You haven't yet seen your partner angry, frustrated, or sad. Before you expose your relationship to the public eye, allow time for some private development. Just like a baby, if that relationship doesn't have a strong immune system, it runs the risk of unnecessary sickness when it encounters others. And this is where many of you have gone wrong. You put your baby (relationship) in too many hands, when it only needed the love and care of those responsible for it.

It can start off okay but can turn into a huge disaster when you let too many people have access too soon. You'll give them a little insight into the relationship and they start giving you all kinds of advice. They feel they should be a part of all your decisions and actions, and need to be updated about everything that's going on. We learned that too many hands in the early stages of dating can be detrimental to a relationship's ability to healthily grow and mature. To be very candid, this was difficult for me and Tasha. We wanted to come out on social media, tell everyone in our friend circle, and even share it at church. But we knew the relationship was too vulnerable; it was too early; it was premature. And although it might have given us instant feelings of affirmation and attention, we realized we were out for something deeper. **If we could endure this short period of establishing a solid foundation in private, we would enjoy a long-term, successful marriage in public.**

2. Trusted Voices/Sources of Accountability

Although you don't want to share the relationship with everyone, you still need some sources of accountability. These are individuals in your life who don't have a hidden agenda or ulterior motive and who want to see the best for you both. These should be individuals who are not immature, controlling, or insecure. They should have a solid relationship, established with much credibility, or should have greatly failed in relationships and can provide wisdom and insight. They should be those who can pray for you, intercede on your behalf, and be unbiased in their approach. Often these are people who can see when the relationship is veering off course, having the sensitivity to see warning signs and discern obstacles down the road that can be avoided. Parents, church leaders, and a strong married couple served in this capacity for Tasha and me. These were people with whom we could let down our guard and be totally transparent. These were people who would be completely honest and tell us the truth about various aspects of our relationship. No relationship should be on an island. Sometimes we can be so deep in love that we need another set of eyes to see objectively and provide balance to our feelings. Never let your relationship be controlled by individuals, but do accept counsel and support with wisdom and love. Although we didn't come to them often or about everything, it was refreshing to know that we had trusted voices accessible to us when we needed them. **They weren't necessarily concerned about our feelings, but committed to our future.**

3 Ways to Build a Strong Foundation

Every solid building needs a strong foundation. Many people get caught up with the aesthetics of a relationship and are overly concerned about the outward appearance. But the foundation of the relationship is where its strength lies. Tasha and I didn't want a relationship that looked good on the outside but was internally void of substance. We didn't want a relationship that would crumble to the ground once a storm came. We didn't want to move too quickly and skip crucial steps in the building process. We wanted stability. We desired to build a strong foundation during the dating phase which would be the platform to building a successful future. This was our focus.

1. Transparent Conversations

We had been dating for about three months and things were going well. We were getting to know each other even better and were ready to dig a little deeper in our level of conversations. I'll never forget sitting down together one night, looking each other in the eye, and saying, "Let's talk about our past." We initiated an open forum to share about our past experiences with dating, relationships, and sexual history. We also opened up about our failures, hurts, and disappointments. This was such a revealing time for us because we got to hear each other express from the fibers of our heart. ***It's impossible to build a great future together without involving each other in your past.*** We decided that we weren't going to hide anything. We wanted to be an open book for each other so that we could build from a place of trust.

One of the greatest failures of any relationship is the inability to be transparent and open in communication. Often the things that we are holding back in the relationship are blocking growth and development. If we don't share them early in the relationship they run the risk of emerging later, with intensified strength. Get it out in the open early and be honest, whatever it might be. Take time to sit down and have the hard conversations. If these things are deal breakers early in the relationship and the other person can't handle them, it will save you from a lot of wasted time. It also allows you time to work through some of these issues together. Avoid keeping secrets. Learn the art of working through things and building a strong foundation together.

We not only had transparent conversations about our past, but also about our future. Early in the relationship we would often discuss where we were going. What did we both want out of life? What were our goals? Aspirations? Occupations and educational goals? How many kids did we want? Where did we want to live? When I met Tasha I understood that she was very passionate about education. She was finishing her Master's degree and planning to pursue her Ph.D. at the University. Through our conversations, I came to understand the time commitment necessary to achieve this goal. She was also interested in teaching at the college level for a short time and doing some work in local community, eventually making an impact at the national level. I also knew that she was passionate about God and serving in ministry. I was confident about her faith in God and that we would always put Him first in each of our decisions which was very refreshing to know! On the flipside, she met me a time when I was accepting my call into ministry. I was also a musician and was basically the second-man in charge in terms of leadership at the church we were attending. One of the things that we discussed early in the relationship was my love for God and my faithfulness to the local church. We were in the midst of a building project and I would spend countless hours working and helping out at church. Although it was challenging at times, I applauded her because she knew from our initial conversations that she was dating a "minister!" And she had to come to grips that this wasn't going to change and would definitely be a major part of our future. It would have been unfair to avoid this conversation early in the relationship and have her figure out the dynamics of who I was later.

Your communication about your past as well as your future is vital to the success of building a strong foundation together!

2.   Establishing a List of Non-Negotiables

Every relationship in the dating phase needs a set of non-negotiables. These are things in the relationship that you agree upon and refuse to compromise. We learned that if certain expectations aren't established and understood early in the relationship, you run a greater risk of compromising them later. What will you not allow? What are you unwilling to accept? What are the boundaries? What are the standards of the relationship? We took time to answer all these questions and didn't wait until they arose to address them. We foresaw various scenarios that could potentially arise in our relationship and set a plan of action. We thought proactively instead of reactively.

So, we both sat down and began to discuss things that were important to the foundation and success of our relationship. One of the things in the forefront was our commitment and relationship with God. We implemented times to fast and pray together, to study, and to consecrate. We made sure that God was priority and was at the core of each of our decisions. Not including God in our daily agenda and affairs wasn't an option. Another major area that we strove not to compromise was pre-marital sex. And oh, was this a tough one! As we spent more time together, the flames of love and passion became more and more difficult to suppress. Although we knew there was a strong possibility that we would spend the rest of our lives together, we still wanted to try to do things the right way and wait until marriage. ***When the door of pre-marital sex is opened in a dating relationship, it establishes a relationship that is more focused on passion than purpose.*** And although passion has its place in any relationship, the goal of the dating phase is to further explore purpose. When passion becomes the focus, heightened feelings and emotions are the captains that drives the ship. And we all know that our feelings and emotions can change. Setting the non-negotiable of no pre-marital sex places the purpose of the relationship as the focus and ensures that it is not overtaken by passion. And being totally transparent with you, this was tough! Very tough! If you don't come together and set some boundaries, it can get totally out of hand. If you have found your relationship is veering off in the zone of passion, simply grab the reigns and re-center it on its purpose.

We implemented practices to reinforce the integrity of what we were building. One of the things we found helpful was do things in groups. Whether with family or mutual friends, doing things in a group setting takes the focus off of your individual relationship and teaches you how to vibe with others around. We often would go to the movies, dinner, out of town, and other places with groups. We also soon found out that we had to limit the late nights, with the sun coming up over our apartments. Late nights alone can lead to a little bit of everything! We didn't allow each other to spend the night and we also respected each other's space during dating. We didn't put ourselves in the place to "play" married. I wasn't her husband, yet and she wasn't yet my wife. We didn't move in together, have keys to each other's place, drive each other's cars, wash each other's clothes, or do any of that married folk stuff. We knew that we would have plenty of time to do that. We kept the focus on building a strong foundation and on learning each other and the God-given purpose in our relationship.

3. Evolving Relationships

Although we were enjoying each other immensely, we began to notice how our relationship was affecting the various relationships around us. Tasha has always been "Ms. Popular," with lots of friends and people around her. When we met, I was introduced to lots of people in her various circles, from her academic circles, to friends and family back home in Chicago, to sorority sisters! I also had a wide range of relationships throughout the community from high school to college, church, musicians and more. Since we were in this newfound relationship, we discovered that it infringed upon time that we would traditionally be spending with other people. How could we balance this relationship so that we were investing time and building together without affecting our relationships with other people? I'll never forget how frequently my wife would travel to Chicago to visit friends and family back home. But when we started dating, some of those people were like, "Tasha, where have you been?" "You've come up missing!" A lot of her time was now spent with me, doing various things together to build the relationship.

The hard truth is that once you are in a serious dating relationship, your other relationships will evolve. Now this is not necessarily a bad thing, but it must be understood. Most of the time these changes won't be forever but are necessary during the period of establishing that strong foundation together. I remember still being a musician, my fellow musicians and I would get together and "shed!" This means coming together and practicing and playing into the wee hours of the night. But when I started dating, the fellas told me I came up missing! They would tease, "Oh you got to check in and can't come, huh?!"

To address this, we established a principle that my friends were her friends, and her friends were my friends. It might sound crazy, but it is proven and it works! Let me explain. Lots of the conflict that many dating couples experience comes because of people outside the relationship. These might be old boyfriends, your girls that you would go out and party with, fellas that you guys would hang with and pick up ladies, or even single friends who simply have a different perspective on dating. If you try to maintain these relationships the way you did before you began dating, they can become a distraction and negatively influence what you are trying to establish. When you are in a serious dating relationship, you might not be able to hang out with the guys every night like you did years ago. You might not be able to take multiple girls' trips every year like you were accustomed to. These relationships must evolve and reflect where you are with your mate. We found ourselves hanging out more with our family, in groups, and around other dating/married couples. We began to mirror what we wanted to see and make positive investments in our future.

Tasha and I came as a package! I introduced Tasha to my close friends, and I met hers. This didn't mean that we forfeited everything we did alone or with our single friends, but there was an understanding, acknowledgement, and respect for what we shared. I just don't believe that you should be in a serious dating relationship and entertain people your mate doesn't know about. What's the secret? Why can't we all be cool? Why can't I meet them?! We didn't have to work extra hard to keep our phones away from each other, nervous about what messages might come through. We established the standard from the beginning to never let outside relationships influence or alter what we were building. **We were together; we were public; and we came as a package!** If you respected me, you respected her. Believe me, it prevented lots of headaches and gave us the foundation we needed to enjoy relationships that were refreshing and complementary to what we shared!

Mirror Moments
Questions

1. How will your future mate benefit from adding you to their life?

2. How often do you spend the day without social media, music, or other noise?

3. In your relationship, who are your trusted voices and sources of accountability?

4. In your relationship, what is your list of non-negotiables?

5. Once you started dating, how have you handled your other evolving relationships?

Mirror Moments

Reflections

Mirror Moments

Reflections

Mirror Moments

Reflections

Mirror Moments

Reflections

3

ENGAGEMENT

Hers

I am a pretty good judge of character. Sometimes this has worked against me. For instance, there are some people I want to be good friends with, but those inner sirens most often tell me to do otherwise. The times I have tried to defy those warnings, I almost always regretted it. Anyway, upon meeting Matthew I immediately knew he was a great guy. However, because I hadn't had much experience in the 'field,' I often thought I needed to avoid appearing too naïve or overly gullible. However, I didn't want to allow my suspecting nature to make me to miss out on a good thing. I tried my best to temper the two dynamics. Ultimately, Matthew was a great person, and someone who I envisioned doing life with.

While my "list" had become a thing of the past, Matthew's love for God, his affectionate nature, and plainly good heart were characteristics that were critical at this stage of my life. Matthew was deeply involved in his church, committed to his family, and was great at balancing time in growing our relationship. His commitment to others often reminded me of myself. If someone around him was launching into an exciting venture, he wanted to be the first to push that person as far as he could. This selfless quality, alongside his true love for God, were the essential components that attracted me.

Our time together was sparse, but very special. Though we lived in a relatively small college town, our conversations were global. His ability to see life beyond the here and now fascinated me. Often, we can become so engulfed with our now, that the future becomes a blur. His ability to dream was a complete turn-on. While I didn't have my entire life mapped out, having someone who hadn't become so content in life was significant for me.

Even at the dating level we began to vision-cast. Before we ever swapped rings, we discussed setting our life plans around building a family and moving to a new state; the fact that those visions have become reality now is astounding.

While I loved mostly everything about him, I needed a few more pieces of evidence that he was sure about moving forward with me. I hadn't dated much, but I was sure that I didn't want to waste time in something that wasn't contributing to my purpose.

It was eight months from the time we started dating until the time I first laid eyes on my engagement ring. I know that's a short amount of time for most, but for me it seemed like an eternity.

Ironically, I was that girl who thought love took time (at least two years). I was skeptical of those who believed in love at first sight. But here I was practically pulling my hair out because I didn't believe that my soon-to-be fiancé was moving swiftly enough in advancing our relationship because though we discussed the future, I still didn't have a ring! It's something about the ring that I learned that made things "official". The public display of love and commitment to one another, through the giving of the ring, was necessary for me. I know nowadays some females propose to their fiancés and take the lead when it comes to taking the relationship to the next level. However, this was one tradition that I wanted to keep intact. Though Matthew didn't always know it, that eight months of dating and waiting was nerve-racking for me.

EMBRACING PROCESS

Historically, when I considered the word love, I always knew it took time. However, when Matthew came on the scene I felt moving forward was the right thing to do without much reservation. Until then, I considered myself a pretty patient person. But there would be a process before I got the ring.

I had to learn to embrace process. Process is defined as "the systematic series of actions directed to some end.[2]" While I knew the end would be marriage, I had a difficult time waiting for his proposal. I had become thirsty – I had an intense desire to progress the relationship without proper perspective[3]. Though we discussed our collective future, I had become frustrated in the process. I thought, "If you love me and want to advance together like you say you do, what's the holdup with my ring, brother?!"

We were driving in the car together and had a very candid conversation about the ring and our engagement. Essentially, I asked the question, "What's the hold up?!" And I remember Matthew calmly responding, "Baby you have to understand that we're headed in that direction, but we aren't quite there just yet!" "WHERE?! We aren't quite where?! What are you talking about?!," I asked. He began to give an analogy of a company manufacturing a particular product, and how even after much consideration, the product doesn't instantaneously go on the shelf. While I understood, and thought the analogy was cute, I still wasn't quite sure how it was applicable to us. What was it we needed to do in order to make it official? He began to explain that products worthy of public consumption

---

[2] According to Dictionary.com.

[3] The constant desire to pursue a relationship without proper perspective.

needed to undergo proper inspection. That sounded real deep to me, but a lot of it began to feel like *game*. Was I being played?!

I walked away from that conversation frustrated. We were planning futures together, spending every allowable moment together, spending countless time in conversation, and had begun adjusting our individual lives to include one another. However, we still hadn't become "official." A majority of our time was spent at church, and because we maintained leadership positions, we were advised to keep our relationship discreet. I had an entered a relationship that would speak of destiny, but it was beginning to feel like a façade.

Boy, this was probably one of the most frustrating times I had ever encountered. I didn't understand the hold up!

Subsequently, one of the most crucial lessons of this season for me was learning about process. You may be at a place in your life where you believe the timing is right, but things have been delayed in manifesting. This can be applied to a relationship, a job advancement, a contract, getting pregnant, or whatever situation you might find yourself in.

3 Essential Components During Process

There are three essential components that aid in embracing process. Firstly, you must understand and apply the art of patience, you must protect the excitement of what you have, and must maintain a solid perspective.

1. Patience

Folks say that patience is a virtue. While I never understood the fullness of that phrase, I know for sure patience isn't something I possessed. However, one of the greatest lessons I needed to learn during the engagement period was patience. I was swift to want to go public because I knew it was right. I had never felt so sure about something in my entire life, but still I had to wait.

Throughout this waiting process, the Lord began to show me about how impulsiveness was an issue for me. However, having to "wait" for Matthew was a great lesson in understanding how God communicated with me. Typically, when God allows me to envision something it usually takes about 12-18-months before it manifests.

2. Protection

Because I didn't get what I wanted right away, I had to maintain a level of maturity and not betray what was meant to bless me.

Sometimes when people don't move at the pace we think they should, we begin to casually entertain discussions with our *comfort corners*[4] about who they are, and begin to philosophize about why they didn't move like we hoped they would. When this happens, we unknowingly allow others to surmise about their level of action or inaction. And because the ones we are casually venting to don't have the same investment in the relationship as us, they won't easily snap back once things are put in perspective. Hence, it is essential that each party protect what you have started to build, even though you may be still at the foundational levels.

3. Perspective

When I first discover something or someone, I'm stupid excited. I tell everyone about it. I sometimes feel the need to let others know that there are still good people in the world, and somehow, I hope to share that wealth. However, the excitement between Matthew and I was the fact that we'd verbally promised each other that we would spend life together. And while I had never undergone an engagement period, I knew the ring would symbolize the evidence of that promise. However, when the ring didn't come soon enough I nearly lost the momentum of my excitement because I failed to keep things in perspective.

Never allow one day or one situation to define the totality of the relationship. Because I didn't get the ring when I wanted it,

---

[4] Those people we keep in our lives who don't contribute much, but have become our places of comfort and refugee when we feel like we need them most.

my mind began to create scenarios: a) maybe he isn't serious about moving forward, b) maybe this is all a joke, c) maybe he isn't who he says he is, d) perhaps there's something he recently discovered about me that he doesn't want to commit to, e)maybe he couldn't afford a ring, f)maybe instead of putting up drywall at the church he's been entertaining someone else and hasn't garnered the guts to tell me…you get the picture. You name it, I considered it! I allowed my perspective to shift from envisioning a life full of joy with my mate alongside me to a life full of uncertainties.

Remaining patient, protecting what you value, and staying focused with perspective are indispensable factors that will strengthen your bond.

The Proposal

Once I got over myself, I was able to live a bit more freely, unfocused on what Matthew would do, when he would do it, and how it would all go down. I'd created a bit of a pattern here: anytime I took my hands off, it allowed God to maneuver in an unrestricted way.

It was May 5, 2006. Exactly five years after I graduated college for the first time. I had worked late that Thursday. One of my middle school students had lost her cell phone. Before I had to face a possibly irate parent, I did everything in my power to diffuse the situation, to no avail. An extra hour and a half badgering middle schoolers about a lost phone was no real fun.

It was typical of Matthew to call as I was leaving work and because I was leaving much later than usual I had a few missed calls from him. We finally connected. I was exhausted but he had expressed interest in going back to revisit a home we viewed previously. We knew we were getting married, and weeks before we'd started looking at homes and considering our future together. We'd fallen in love with one particular condo we'd seen online. It was owned by an older guy named Don. Don was incredibly nice but after putting his home on the market, he decided not to move after all. However, his decision came after we fell in love with the space. The square footage was amazing, and it had a balcony that overlooked the water.

So Matthew called me and told me he was leaving work and wanted to know where I was. He told me he wanted to see the place one more time. Though I was unsettled at the fact that Don decided to no longer sell the place, I too wanted to get one last look, so I headed over. Matthew had arrived before me. Instead of waiting in his truck so we could enter together, Matthew was already upstairs. I shook my head and went up the stairs. Once I made it to the top, I rang the bell. Don welcomed me with glee and I could see Matthew had pretty much made himself comfortable inside. I said, "Hey babe!" There was something different in his eyes that day. Don drifted into the background, and it was if he'd left Matthew and me in the condo alone. Matthew took me near the balcony and on the table I saw a red rose and a ring box! Immediately I knew what was happening! On the one hand I was in a state of shock! On the other hand, I was embarrassed that I had been tricked. I also saw Matthew's nervousness as he went down on one knee. I was so sure about this that I wanted to save him the fear of a possible rejection and nearly wanted to skip the formalities. He went through with it and there I was, utterly flabbergasted. Almost on cue, Don appeared with wine glasses poured for each of us. I could not believe that he was in on it too! It was happening! I was getting married, for real! WOW!!! Shortly afterward the pomp and circumstance, we graciously thank Don for allowing us to create a memory that included him and his beautiful place. We drove my car home, and I will never forget that feeling of relief that marriage was finally happening for a girl like me!

The Engagement Party

Because I was away at graduate school, I lived away from home. So, in order for most of my family and close friends to meet Matthew, I wanted to have an engagement party. During that time our families would mingle and gel for the first time. We did it in Chicago. It was an amazing time.

For the first time we gathered both sides of our families and our closest friends. We wanted to present to our families and friends what we were doing. And while a great majority of the people who attended the engagement party had not yet met Matthew, I wanted them to come to witness the love I often spoke about.

There was plenty of food, lots of laughs and there was our first merging of our families and friends together. I had heard so many stories about crazy in-laws and had a bit of anxiety about how it would all work out. Each person in our families came from different backgrounds. However, the connection between our respective families seemed effortless.

ENGAGEMENT
His

No Wasting Time

Dating Tasha was simply amazing! Things were just different with her, different than any other relationship I had experienced. During our time dating, I really got a chance to discover who she was. I loved spending time with her. I was intrigued by her. Our conversations seemed effortless, where we openly shared our hearts on God, our purpose, and how much we wanted out of life. I wanted to be around her more and more, and I hated when we had to leave each other's presence. I wanted more. I wanted the next level. I saw our power individually but saw the greater potential of us together. I was convinced that this was the woman that I wanted to spend the rest of my life with.

I had come to the place in my life where I was ready to make a whole-hearted commitment. And in this day and age, that word is almost like a cuss word! Nobody wants to be committed. It seems everyone is after a temporary fix and can only see what's before them today, neglecting the promise of their tomorrow. I was committed to move beyond my feelings of today and catapulted me into the power of my future. I had experienced so much dysfunction in relationships that I was ready to experience the fullest of what a real relationship was.

I had found that in Tasha. Why would I blow this moment? Why wouldn't I walk into the new level for this relationship whole-heartedly? Why would I limit the relationship to merely dating, when I knew there was more? I refused to let my history infringe upon my future. I wasn't going to let my past, fear, insecurity, uncertainty, or any other negativity push me away from one of the greatest seasons of my life. You could be reading this book and could be on the brink of your NEXT! Whatever that next is for you. Don't back up or talk yourself out of it. Sometimes we think things are too good to be true. We can be so programmed to things going "wrong" that we become numb to really embracing when things are "right." When God flips your life and brings what you have prayed for, don't block the blessing by wasting valuable time!

I remember having a conversation with my dad about Tasha. I told him, "Dad, I really think that she is the one, and I wanna propose to her." He looked at me and said, "Son, what are you waiting on? I am behind you." And those were words that I took to heart. It provided a resolve to some of the questions that I had in my head. Because I knew she was the one, I wanted to propose, and I wanted to spend the rest of my life with her. But I didn't want to appear as if I was moving too fast. I didn't want to be rushing it. In hindsight, I was comparing my relationships to what I had seen in other people. Most people I knew dated for many years and knew each other for a long time. They might have attended college together or had been high school sweethearts. I had only known Tasha for approximately 8 months – less than a year! What would people say? What would people think? It was in the few minutes of conversation with my father that he brought things into proper perspective. It didn't matter what anyone else thought about it. Often, we can be controlled by the opinions of others and paralyzed at the place of decision. Now I am not telling you to neglect calculating the cost and making a sound decision, because I did all of that. But what I am saying is that when God gives you the green light, everyone else's opinion must yield to God's yes. I knew that God had orchestrated this and the confirmation from my father and Pastors gave me the confidence to not waste any more time!

How I knew Tasha was my Wife

A lot of people ask me the question, "How did you know that she was the one?" There were so many reasons, but I want to compress them into 5 ways that I knew Tasha was my wife:

1.   She was a God-lover

I had met a woman that loved God for real. Not a woman who just liked to go to church or who considered herself to be religious, but one that had relationship with God! When I met her she already had a solid relationship with God and was passionate about strengthening it. Her focus was on a vertical relationship with God, before pursuing a horizontal relationship with anyone else. She wasn't devoting any time looking for a man. Her focus wasn't throwing herself on me, but she was settled and positioned to be found. She wasn't looking for me. And that was huge! It always was a turn off to me to have the woman pursing me. She wasn't a woman who was going to do the work of the man in pursuing a relationship, but she was confident to remain in a position to be pursued. I also loved the fact that she never said, "God told me" or "God showed me." I had experienced this before in relationships, where women would tell me that God said I was their husband. WHAT?! How is God going to tell you that and never shares that with me? Many women use this as a form of control or as bait to reel the man into some mystical spiritual awareness or something. Lol. Even if God shows the woman, she should never reveal or voice this to the man before he affirms and confirms his intent. It should never be used as the leading voice, but as a confirming one.

2.   She established standards and disciplines

When I met Tasha and we started dating, I noticed that she already had standards and disciplines in place. She didn't wait to meet me to start them. Her life was structured with certain standards that she implemented on her own. One of the things that I noticed was that she was very classy. She was a woman. She didn't feel the need to advertise her body or wear revealing clothing. She also wasn't overly flirtatious or provocative. She had old school values with a new school perspective. I could tell that she came from good stock and had embraced people who had much wisdom. She also was an avid reader, studier, and researcher. She was a lover of knowledge and wasn't limited in perspective or ability to continue to learn and grow. She also kept a clean apartment and car, and liked nice things. She had very solid credit and was a huge giver! She was a tither, offering giver, and was found helping and blessing people all the time. She was also very health conscious; when I met her she had been vegan for five years. I wasn't in any way thinking about that lifestyle at all! But it revealed a lot about her ability to embrace a holistic approach to wellness in not only her eating, but in many areas of her life.

3. She had clear goals and a vision for her life

I met Tasha while she was completing her Master's degree at the University. She had gone through some adversity, but still maintained her focus and passion to complete what she started. That spoke volumes. She wasn't waiting on a man to come into life before she got her stuff together. Her stuff was already in place! Her goals in life were established, from education, to ministry, to business and career. She had a vision for her life and wasn't living life haphazardly without direction. She knew where she was going. She had a sense of direction. She had discovered her purpose in life and was confident in who God had made her. Some people don't start dreaming and living until they meet their mate. But that is very dangerous, because your goals and dreams in life can't be solely contingent on another person. There are some things that you must do in life for YOU. Having someone else to share them with should only enhance what's already there! You can't give anyone goals. You can't tell someone else their purpose. You can blow passion into someone. These things are innate and must be brought to the table. Tasha had them!

4. She was committed to supporting my dreams

During our many conversations, I revealed my passion and dreams to Tasha. It was so refreshing to watch her eyes light up as I shared my heart. She was a great listener and hung on to every word that I shared. She then would share with me ideas, creative insights, and an overall perspective of support. At the time, my application to graduate school had recently been rejected. I'll never forget her saying, "Don't be discouraged, because if that didn't work, there must be another avenue that God wants you take." We researched and explored other programs, and she was committed to seeing my dreams flourish.

I also watched her support me in things that she didn't quite understand fully. I was a huge part of the launch of a ministry, and that took lots of my time. A whole lot! There were nights when I would be at the church for hours on end. There were weeks where I would see the church more than I would see my own apartment. Although we were dating, it was clear that the work of the ministry and the church was huge to me. It would take some adjustment, but even through this she was committed and supportive.

5.   She understood the power of Unity

It was great to know what we each brought to the table, but it was more powerful knowing what we could accomplish together. ***She was good at being "her" and I was good at being "me," but she embraced the idea of "we."*** She really understood who she was but had an awesome ability to respect who God had called me to be as well. This unlocked the great potential of who we could be together. She wanted to do this thing called life together. If we were hurt, we were going to be hurting together. If we were broke, we were going to be broke together. If we were at the optimal level of success, we would experience it together. She understood that we were more powerful and much greater, together. Having a woman know that is everything.

The Proposal

It was in May of 2006 that I decided that I wanted to make things official and propose to Tasha. At this point I had met her mother and most of her family in Chicago. We had a great vibe, and I was confident that everyone would be in support of my decision. Tasha had also been around my family throughout most of our relationship, and everyone was in favor of my decision to move forward with the proposal.

So, the first thing on the list was to find a ring. To be honest, I really wasn't sure what I was looking for! I just observed Tasha's taste and wanted to make sure that it was a ring that caught the eye! I knew she liked nice things and wanted this ring to be a statement of the love that I had for her. I shopped around a few places over the course of three weeks, but really couldn't find a ring that I wanted. I was considering getting a ring custom made, but was hoping that I could find something already made at one of the jewelry stores in our town. It was on a Friday around noon, during the last week of April that I visited Rogers and Hollands jewelry store in the mall for the first time. I talked to the manager and explained the kind of ring that I wanted. I walked around the store and there was one that really caught my eye. It was double-banded with diamonds all around it, with a princess cut diamond in the center. I knew that it would meet her standards and be something that she could wear for years to come. I told the manager, "That's the one." I was a little nervous because I wasn't sure how much it cost. She got the ring out of the case and flipped over the price tag…I just stood there as she told me its dollar amount! At the time I was working at a radio station and had a saved a few dollars, but I hadn't saved that much! Goodness! Nevertheless, I just had a great feeling about the ring, and wanted to finalize things that day, but wanted to be 100% sure. I definitely didn't want Tasha to see the ring before the proposal or even know that I was ring shopping. I needed a second option!

I decided to call our friend Janiele. I asked her where she was and if she could come to the mall really quick. She was one of the people I could confide in about the engagement, and when I told her I had found the ring she said, "Okay, Matthew! Let me take my lunch. I'm on my way." I stayed in the store and started working out pricing with the manager to made sure I got the best deal possible. In a matter of minutes Janiele was there. I told her to give me her honest opinion of the ring. The manager took it out of the case, wiped it off, and showed it to her. I'll never forget her face when she saw it. She said, "Dang!! Matt this NICE! It's HOT…You balling, mug!" That was all I needed to hear. I made the purchase that day.

Surprising Tasha was a very difficult task. I had tried a few times before and it was very hard to get something past her without her finding out. At the time we were fascinated with looking at homes and visiting open houses in the area. She had seen a very nice condo online and wanted me to view it with her. We had seen it once and wanted to view it again. She was still at work and wanted me to meet her over at the place to view it after she got off. I arrived before her and walked in the condo. It was beautiful! It was had an amazing view of the lake from the balcony. The day was sunny and the ambiance was beautiful. This was where I wanted to propose. When I told the owner what I wanted to do, and he was totally okay with it! He told me, "Go for it!" So, I ran to the car and grabbed the ring and sat out on the balcony. By this time, Tasha was calling me to ask if I had arrived. I told her that I was already in the condo and that she could just come on up. She got there about five minutes later and was rushing up the steps, excited to see the place. She rang the doorbell and the owner greeted her and let her in. My heart was pumping. She asked if I was there, and the owner led her back to the balcony. She seemed puzzled as to why I was on the balcony. I immediately greeted her and gave her a hug. I held her hand and begin to get on my knees to propose. I was so nervous, it was crazy! I had thought of some of the words that I wanted to say, but it was like my whole world just slowed down! My palms were sweating and I don't even remember what I was saying. I remember her looking at me like, "Ask me!!" Finally, I got the words out, "Will you marry me?!" She pulled me up by the hand and with tears in her eyes said "YES, baby!"

By this time, the owner and his wife had set out another chair, had wine glasses in their hands, and were popping open a bottle of wine. They clapped and congratulated us! They left us alone and we sat out on the balcony, looking over the lake, and just enjoying this moment. It was one of the most amazing feelings I ever had. I felt so light! It was official: I asked, and she said yes! We were getting married!

Mirror Moments
Questions

1. What do you believe are the major barriers preventing your relationship from going to the next level?

2. How do you know your soon-to-be-spouse is the one?

3. Do you truly believe you're ready to be married?

4. Have you established a working relationship with your potential in-laws?

5. Can you imagine your life without your potential spouse?

Mirror Moments

Reflections

Mirror Moments

Reflections

Mirror Moments

Reflections

Mirror Moments

Reflections

4

MARRIAGE

It was six o'clock in the evening on October 14, 2006. This was this that day we decided to share with the rest of the world and celebrate our union. It was a powerfully charged day. We had nearly 500 of our closest friends and family packed in the sanctuary. Typically, the bride-to-be leads in the vision of what the day looks like. She is the one who pick out the colors, establishes the program, and orchestrates all the various components and details of the day. But our wedding was different. We started off with so much unity and dedicated the same time and energies to how we wanted to plan our wedding. Matthew was so instrumental in this day and wanted it to be top notch! Our course, I wanted this day to be an unforgettable display of the love and union that we shared. Our collaboration was amazing. We wanted it to be beautiful and elegant, but we also wanted it to be one where the presence of God and the expression of this covenant was felt. We started the ceremony with praise and worship and liturgical dancers. There was a full band that accompanied, with some of the region's best vocalists in place. It was electrically charged, and the spirit of joy and celebration filled the room. The ceremony was so Spirit-filled that Matthew and some of the other groomsmen and bridesmaids "shouted" and danced. We had a beautiful rendition of the Lord's Prayer sung, and we shared communion together, sealing this amazing bond!

We had planned to have the reception at the newest Hilton hotel in town. However, two weeks prior to the wedding we got word that the construction was delayed! By this time, nearly 1000 invitations had already been sent out. We had a conversation about it but stayed calm believing that it would be worked out. The staff at the Hilton called around and made us aware that every possible venue within a 20-mile radius was already booked. Finally, the staff concocted a plan and made reservations to hold our reception after hours at a historic mall in the neighboring city. The venue was squared away but we now had to consider how we would feed our guests. We had a three-course meal planned when we were at the original location, but we now had to figure out how to pull it off in a location not equipped with a full-service kitchen. We began to pool together our resources. Because we were in the third month of owning a restaurant together, we decided we could use our catering services to serve us! So, guess what? We flipped our reception from an elegant three-course menu to a down home spread! We had fried chicken (with Chicago-style mild sauce), fried fish, macaroni and cheese, and all the trimmings! It wound up being a hit! We got a chance to take lots of pictures and mingle with guest from far and near!

We had an amazing time, but we were truly exhausted! We rested the next day (Sunday) and packed for our honeymoon to Freeport, Bahamas on Monday. We spent five nights exploring life together. We swam, played tennis in the sweltering heat, ventured out into the local community, snorkeled for the first time, made good love, and were amazed about the endless possibilities that life together would offer.

We flew back home and turned the key to our new place and began to navigate life in marriage. We had witnessed many beautiful weddings and exotic honeymoons that only ended in failed marriage. We were determined to create something different.

Modeled Marriage

Families are an essential component for any thriving community. Since the inception of slavery, it has been evident that to intercept the connectedness of a family is to disrupt a community. When families are broken, it's nearly impossible for communities to thrive. Communities are built through marriages which ultimately become strong families. Marriages are the bedrock of any successful community, because they create within them a dualistic pairing of purposes and passions. These pairings nurture children by equipping them with the tools to become not only productive citizens, but to become owners of their identities, ultimately allowing them to understand what their individual contribution to the world should be.

From the time Matthew and I started dating, I prayed one prayer: "Lord, give us a modeled marriage." I did not know the fullness of that prayer, but I wanted to have something that people could look to. I wanted to have a marriage that people could model their own marriages after. I wanted to create something with Matthew that was real, that was fun, but not so far-fetched that people couldn't think that true joy in marriage could be attained. I wanted something that I didn't have to fake. I wanted something that was enjoyable. I wanted to help create a union that inspired people to believe in love again. I wanted to do marriage right!

However, considering my background, and not having much practice at relationships, I didn't know how this would eventually come to pass. My mom was divorced. My grandparents lived separately. I never saw an actual model of what I so fervently hoped for.

While it was the most exciting time of my entire life, there still existed an internal fear that what I hoped would grow would actually die, like many examples I had seen. Or worse, what if I had signed up for a dead-end situation? I knew far too many women who had felt trapped in unending cycles of unhappiness and in dungeons of depression and despair. I had nothing to prove to anybody, but I wanted to make my wait worth it! I truly believed God desires marriages to work. I still believed that the institution created by God to impact a thriving community was possible, even if it wasn't always easy. What we would ultimately create would have to be God-given.

The start of this journey of marriage was so exciting for me! I had finally found the love of my life. We had an amazing wedding and shared an unbelievable connection during our honeymoon. I realized that these were two major events, but I wanted to create this within our daily lives. I was 100% dedicated to making our marriage the best marriage that it could be. Although I knew that solid and healthy marriages weren't formed overnight, I was ready to roll up my sleeves and put in the work.

One of my motivations was the divorce of my parents. I have two amazing and God-fearing parents. They did such a great job raising my brothers and me, instilling in us some principles that we could apply in all areas of life. And although my parents were both amazing people, they divorced in my teenage years. Later in life, I was able to process this fully. The major takeaway was that **this was not necessarily a reflection of who they were individually, but an outcome of who they failed to be together.** This newfound perspective really put things in place for me. Although you can have two great people individually, it still requires work to make them two great people together. Tasha and I were both solid people separately; we both loved God and put Him first, had crazy potential in life, and mind-blowing dreams and vision for our lives. But we now had to merge these things and be great together! This is where many people fail. It's not easy. Over 50% of marriages end in divorce. Divorce was not an option for me! I didn't want to become a statistic. I looked around and saw some effective marriages, but really didn't see the example close-up. I was determined to ensure our relationship was the definition of the marriage that I wanted to see. I refused to waste some of the failures I witnessed throughout the years. I counted them as blessings; now I could use my God-given wisdom as a guide to make this thing called marriage work!

KEY AREAS OF DISCUSSION FOR SUCCESS IN MARRIAGE

For the remainder of this book, we want to highlight significant areas in marriage that we believe can make or break the relationship. In this section, instead of the "hers" and "his" sections previously outlined, we take a collective approach to represent the unity of marriage. In this chapter we discuss: marriage identity, communication, balance, and provide keys to maintaining a fresh and thriving union.

MARRIAGE IDENTITY

About a year into our marriage, I remember deciding that instead of changing, I wanted out! Nothing drastic happened, it was simply a much easier option. I had devised a plan. I found a divorce letter online and tweaked it to my standards. I had made up my mind that I would send it to my husband via email. Before pressing the send button, I knew for sure that the marriage deserved a fight, but I was too lazy and unwilling to give of myself in a way that required sacrifice. Wait, did I already mention this? Marriage is not for the selfish! I was selfish. I focused on my needs, my desires, my levels of comfort. I was all about me!!!! I can't remember the instance, but I know for sure it was a time in our marriage that challenged me to look in the mirror and take corrective action in order to make our marriage better. But I was willing to take the road most traveled: a divorce.

I sent the letter. My husband received it but gave it very little time or energy. I knew he deleted it. Even though I knew his mother and father had experienced that, I somehow felt he would agree that in some cases divorce is just necessary. I was pitiful. I was looking to receive empathy from a place where I wasn't willing to give much of anything. Super selfish!

From the beginning, I knew marriage was not for chumps! Chumps in my book are those who are easily discouraged, who lack the wherewithal to fight. They are the opposite of champs! Prior to marriage, I never understood divorce. But after only a few months in, I soon realized that it was so easy to not remain married. And while nothing life-altering happened to trigger it, at times I considered dissolving our marriage. In those moments, I wasn't ready to become who I needed to be for my husband. I was selfish.

Anyway, my plans for a divorce lasted about an hour. Well, I really didn't have a plan at all aside from the fact that I had hoped to use the letter as a scare tactic, one that would somehow cause my husband to back off me and allow me to continue in my selfishness. It didn't work! The night passed and we never even spoke of it again.

Once I was done with these shenanigan, I understood that marriage wasn't a time for playing and trying little tricks. It was a place where we would explore love in a way that exemplified commitment. We understood that neither of us came to the place of marriage as perfect individuals, but what we needed to improve, we would work on us, collectively. Divorce is a word we never spoke again.

Developing Non-Negotiables

Non-negotiables would become the things that we would never allow flexibilty. These became things that were never up for discussion. Divorce become one of them. And ultimately, we decided that we would work through life together come hell or high water, and divorce would never be a viable option. **Side note**: Sometimes many believe marriage means a problem free life, so when problems come they opt for divorce. However, marriage doesn't mean you won't face battles. It just means you have someone who is committed to fighting with you to ensure victory.

Some of our other non-negotiables are included in the list below:

1. Commit to growth so divorce will never be an option

While divorce is biblically allowable or permissible when the spouse dies or when adultery becomes a factor, many use it as a cop out. Now, our stance is not that marriage is easy, but it is not for the faint of heart. If you think getting married is going to cure your woes, or possibility serve as the medium from which all joy evolves, you are sadly mistaken. Many pursue marriage because they fear being alone. Or they are pressured by those around them to couple up. However, if the proper perspective of marriage is not kept in take, divorce easily becomes the most viable solution. We are not suggesting remaining in an abusive relationship, or putting one's life at stake, but good marriages take tremendous work.

On the other hand, I have seen people stay together just for the sake of staying together. Their joy was lost two days after the wedding. The responsibility of raising children has worn them out. The lack of time spent with their overworked spouse has been a source of constant contention, yielding no lasting change. And soon, one year turns into 20 and the spouses have merely become roommates. Essentially, the only growth is in the space that separates them.

Healthy marriages are worth working and fighting for! It is important that there is a mutual commitment made and decided upon that fuses the bond to weather the storms that will surely come.

2. That we were committed to protecting our marriage

While marriage is awesome, there are days it won't be. However, there must be a maturity between both parties that agrees that though things are bad between us, we are committed to protecting what we share. Many are so immature that when they get upset at their spouses, they take to social media, or to their friends or comfort corners. On the spiritual side of things, when you allow doors to open and darts to be shot at your spouse, the impact of the darts remain long after the fight is over.

I remember when Matthew and I were just getting serious. Because I was new to town, there were countless people who knew him much longer than I did. A few individuals attempted to use their history with him as power over my relationship with him. I quickly decided that no one could violate him in my presence. And while insight can sometimes be beneficial, *I quickly decided their history had nothing to do with our destiny*.

3. Refusing to handle private conflicts publicly

This was essential for us. Privacy, though a lost art, is the essence of true relationships. Relationships are personal. Hence, your interactions in your relationships should be, too. When you argue in public, it gives spectators permission to disrespect your union. And while you and your mate will eventually kiss and make up, the respect you lost publicly is hardly ever fully recoverable.

4. Our marriage would be defined by unity

With the demands of life, it takes intentional effort to stay together. Early on, we decided that we would do life together. This meant, that we were a package deal. If I was required to be some place, Matthew (if he didn't have a previous commitment) would be there (with our children as well). And the same went for me with him. When we saw one, you saw all! And while this seems simple, we've found that it minimizes the impact of outside elements and people negatively influencing our union.

5. We would celebrate our anniversary childfree

When kids are factored into a relationship, they easily become the focus. However, just because kids have entered the picture, it doesn't give either spouse permission to stop being a husband or wife. I remember one of my friends mentioned, "I hope I never become an amazing mother and horrible wife." That stuck with me. It expressed to me that it would take work to ensure that I wasn't 'succeeding' in one area while neglecting the other. And intentional planned vacations and getaways helped renew what "we" shared between us, especially on the anniversary of "our" union.

6. Our marriage wouldn't be prescribed by roles

The traditions of American society suggest that the woman should take care of the home and the kids while the husband provides monetarily. And while this works for some, we try to remain conscious not to overwhelm each other. For example, if Matthew has cooked dinner for five consecutive days, I can't get lazy and just enjoy the fruit of "his" labor, I need to be intentional by making sure he can kick his feet up on the sixth and seventh day of that week or at least be sure to do the dishes! And vice versa. I shouldn't have to help with homework five days a week; he is sensitive enough to chip in and say, "Hey babe, you go get your nails done, I'm doing homework help today!" These are just small examples, but these kinds of things help ensure that the other knows that "I want to lighten your load, I love you. I got this! I got you!"

7. The more intimacy the better

Intimacy in marriage is a no-brainer. However, with the demands of life, we've found that it takes intentional effort, especially during highly stressful periods, to ensure that we stay connected. We've found that when our schedules are demanding, often the last things on our minds is the intimacy. Because intimacy is our highest form of communication, we often must decide, "You know what, this can wait. I need you!" And intimacy doesn't always mean sex; just sitting by one another (even if you both have laptops open), holding hands, trading quick kisses, back rubs, quick massages, and studying alongside each other all reinforce the love you share.

COMMUNICATION

Communication is the single most important component of any healthy relationship. Especially in marriage, it is imperative that each spouse is willing to express the transparency of their hearts. It is the cornerstone of every relationship, acting as a branch that reaches to every other component. Many relationships fail because they never sufficiently master this key area. It's possible to be in a relationship for years without a true understanding the depths of your spouse's desires. We knew the importance of effective communication and wanted to commit to finding out what worked for our union. This did not happen overnight, and we quickly discovered that it would take constant, intentional effort and attention.

Many spend years hoping to find their "soul mates." This is an innate hope that we will all ultimately find someone, that one, who was specifically designed for us. That one who can, without much explaining, provide for us emotionally, and connect with us spiritually at a level that surpasses anyone else. While this isn't a bad thing to hope for, I do believe many go into marriage and often wind up disappointed because the "magic" they expected to happen either didn't last beyond the honeymoon, or never appeared at all.

A soulmate is, "a person with whom one has a strong affinity, shared values and tastes, and often a romantic bond.[5]" While most of these things were true of Matthew for me, the greatest thing marriage offered me is my *Mirror Mate*. I learned early on that marriage was a revealer. When you are married, the person is there to help you learn and grow; that person becomes not so much a soulmate, but a *Mirror Mate*. A mirror mate is the one who has the ability to reflect love, but more than that, they help bring to surface the areas that are not so loving. **And because many of us are not taught that marriage is a place where growth happens, we flee before things can truly take flight.** It's understandable though, because growth doesn't feel good. It's an intense time of challenging yourself or being challenged by your partner, to become different, become better.

---

[5] According to Dictionary.com

There are three critical areas that were important for me as a wife. 1) Being willing to unlearn & adjust, 2) understanding that silence creates space and 3) that selfishness must be sacrificed.

1. Being Willing to Unlearn & Adjust

I believe people generally are good. We do the right thing and largely are of a good moral conscious. Even so, there are some things we must improve. As a single person, a majority of my quirks didn't immediately harm others. In fact, they often were not perceived as things that needed changing because no one challenged me to do so. I'm not sure if you've heard the saying, "you never truly know a person until you've lived with them." Well, after getting married I understood that fully. We all have areas that we can improve in, but I hadn't changed in forever. I was used to doing things my way. They worked for me! However, because marriage is a revealer, Matthew, as my *Mirror Mate* reminded me of how much I still needed to change. Communication was one of the primary areas where I needed growth. I was accustomed to surface-level encounters. Marriage, however, moves beyond the surface and explores the depths of one's desires.

What does that mean? I was a person who harbored. If something happened in our relationship that I didn't necessarily like, I would process it and reprocess it but much of the time I would not speak on the issue. And if I had previously brought it up, I would sum it up in my mind like such: "Evidently it's something he doesn't deem important because it happened again." And because of that, I would begin to develop philosophies and ideologies about the kind of person he was or was not. I said it all, "Oh, he isn't sensitive to needs of women. Oh, he grew up with two brothers and not sisters, so he doesn't know how to treat a woman." And because I had made peace with how he was, it subconsciously gave me permission to continue in my ways. However, my psychological diagnosis was not beneficial to a healthy union. Hence, I had to unlearn this behavior. I could no longer diagnose, but had to take the time to learn to effectively discuss issues. This took some time!

Every time something went wrong, I couldn't continue to wax philosophical about the kind of person he was. I had to become vulnerable and share my heart. I mean, even simple stuff like: "Babe, that hurt me. Babe, that made me feel this way. Babe, I don't think you're paying attention" and so on. It put me out there! When understanding the core of this, it was because I was prideful. This pride did not allow me to risk my feelings. What if he turned a deaf ear? What if my concerns were deemed invalid? What if I was being immature and petty? When I got to the core of all of this, I began to understand that I was being selfish. Pride is self-centered. However, healthy marriages are the space in which two selfless people thrive.

After all, I wanted the model marriage. Soon, I had to learn to pull my weight. I had to learn to communicate and do it effectively. I wasn't always outright vocal, but I had to do something and do it quickly.

As a naturally observant personality, I would contemplate more than converse. It worked for me as a single person to a certain degree, however this wasn't always beneficial or fruitful in marriage. Further, as a natural writer and researcher, I wasn't always comfortable with face-to-face discussions, so I had to discover news ways to get my point across. So, many times, I would write letters to my husband. Writing was cathartic for me. It allowed me a space to release and no longer harbor my concerns. It allowed me to be myself. More than that, it opened new outlets of communication. While this was different from what Matthew had probably experienced before, it was my most effective means of expression.

But even writing out my feelings wasn't enough; I had to talk with my husband at some point. I remember several conversations where my only contributions were, "Well, I don't know!" Conversations advance relationships, however my "I don't know; I'm not sure" served as certain dead ends. If I wanted to create this model that I had hoped for, and if I wanted a relationship that would live, I HAD to CHANGE! Matthew was so patient: he sometimes endured 24-48 hours periods of silence from me. This time allowed me time to process and actually gain an understanding of what I was truly feeling and how I would say it. I'm thankful he received it so well. I sometimes I still write to express my feelings, but I am much more comfortable talking with my husband. I had to learn that in our marriage, my voice mattered and adding my voice to the conversation of our marriage was necessary.

Maybe ineffective communication is not your thing. My point here is having the flexibility and the heart to adjust in whatever area necessary to grow and advance your relationship. Not everything you do is right. Be flexible and take time to understand ways that you can improve in order to have a more powerful union.

2. Silence Creates Space

When I would go into my diagnostic mode, when I was doing more thinking than expressing, I would find that the gap between us widened. We became more distant. Where we would naturally flow in conversation or household routines, the silence created a wedge. So even though I hadn't verbalized much, many times it was evident that something had intercepted our normal flow. I found the longer it took to correct things, the longer it took to fill the space that I had created between us. Eventually, I discovered that the gaps were not worth it. These spaces represented a space of valuable time, and I did not want to waste our time together.

The gaps lessened, but it took a concerted and intentional

effort on my part to change. I had to adjust and unlearn my way, because LaTasha's way didn't work for the Nesbitts. What might have been a way of life in singlehood could ultimately cause death to a marriage.

3. Selfishness Must Be Sacrificed

Usually, males don't take the lead with communication. However, Matthew came to our relationship raring and ready to go! He was an amazing communicator! He knew exactly what he felt, he knew what he wanted, and he didn't have a problem expressing it to me! Me, on the other hand...not so much. I needed to learn that marriage was a selfless act. It wasn't about my level of comfort. It wasn't fully about my need to contemplate and process my feelings and desires. Marriage and communication had to be about the need to ensure that what we were endeavoring to create would thrive. I had to ensure that I was not committed to comfort, but to change.

It sounds cliché, but change *is* difficult! I couldn't afford to debate whether his style was wrong or mine right; I had to focus on growth. My *Mirror Mate* reminded me that the ball was in my court, so to speak. It was a hard reality. I was far from perfect, but I would not excuse my behavior (or lack thereof) with the infamous alibi of, "This is just how I am." Though it would have been easy to do, I understood that I needed to change for US!

It was all about me. Perhaps it was because I'd had a father and grandfather who provided me everything I thought I needed, and then some. Those same things were evident issues in my marriage. But one of the foundational principles of a truly healthy marriage is becoming so concerned about the other person that your own needs come last. That took some time to learn. **Healthy marriages, or model marriages, are comprised of individuals who are so entrenched and in tune with the needs of their spouse that their own desires are always secondary**. If you aren't ready to put your level of comfort on the backburner, you aren't fully ready for marriage.

My lack of effective communication was comfortable for me. However, if not corrected, this selfish act could have ultimately led to the demise of the greatness God wanted to build in our marriage.

॰

The first few years of our marriage were fun and exciting…but boy, did it take lots of work! I honestly thought that we were gonna come to together and just click from the start, but deep down I knew it would be a process. Think about it: two different people who are used to living independently; two upbringings, two backgrounds, and two different lifestyles. Merge them together in marriage and now they are living under the same roof, trying to figure things out. She likes the heat on 80 degrees at night and the covers off; I like it a little cooler and to add covers as needed. She likes her toast made in the oven; I cook mine on top of the stove. She likes an uncluttered bedroom floor, and I like to create piles so I know where everything is. She likes to go grocery shopping for a few weeks at a time, I like to buy dinner for tonight and come back to the store tomorrow! She likes to fill up the gas tank in both cars, and I like putting in $10, enough to get me through until the next day. LOL!

I consider myself a little different than the average guy. My communication style is rare, I guess. I love to communicate. I like the idea of sitting down together, ironing things out and getting an understanding. I don't care if it's early in the morning or in the wee hours of the night. I don't care if it's in person or over the phone. I am committed to talking it out and getting an understanding in whatever area we are addressing. I really dislike sitting on stuff until the morning. I don't like sweeping stuff under the rug and addressing it months later. My goal in communication is to address issues as they arise, so that we can continue to be on the same page, together. My wife would get a preview of this while we were dating, but she really got to see it up-close once we were married and living together.

I soon discovered that my wife's style of communication was different from mine. Although I considered her an effective communicator, she often would not engage in communication until she had time to fully process the situation. Now sometimes she could be very direct and straight forward, but other times she would get silent and take hours or even a day to fully process things before she talked. There were many times early in our marriage where she went silent. She was still present, but it was like she was thinking about something. She would start to slow down in her engagement and interaction and get kind of quiet. When I would try to find out what happened, she would only say, "Nothing." And oh boy, this was frustrating for me. No matter how I would pry, she wouldn't share her feelings until she could properly process how and why she was feeling that way. This taught me a major lesson about communication early in the relationship: both parties might consider themselves great communicators but possess different communication styles.

We were both committed to communication, but we had two different ways of achieving it. This didn't make one better than other - just different. You might be reading this section thinking that your spouse doesn't communicate. Yes, they do! You just need to uncover HOW they communicate. My style of communication is more instant and spontaneous. My wife's is more contemplative and takes a little more time. Mastering communication requires that each individual acknowledge their style of communication and effectively work to merge both, so that healthy communication is achieved.

Here are 3 tools I used to help facilitate better communication with my wife:

1.   Gentle Reminders

Nobody likes being nagged. In many relationships, the wife is the initiator of communication and finds herself nagging at her counterpart: "You're not talking to me!" "When are you going to get that done?" Generally, the other person gets annoyed and shuts down or either lashes out in an unhealthy way. Remember that the goal is not to create more problems with your communication, but to develop an understanding and a solution.

When my wife didn't want to talk, I learned to stop pressing so hard. Early in the marriage, I would press and pry and ask, "Why aren't you talking?" I would constantly come to her saying, "You know we've got to talk this through." This wasn't working! This wasn't pushing her to talk to me or to open up at all. In hindsight, it might have caused her to close down even more and distracted her from processing her thoughts. So instead, I would tell her that I was available and opened to chat when she was ready to talk. I also found it helpful to give her gentle reminders. Not nagging, but letting her know that her voice was important, and that I didn't forget that we still needed the time and space for her to share. Those gentle reminders were everything! They let her know that her feelings were important and deserved my time and attention. I wanted to let her know that I didn't forget and that I valued her ability to share, sooner rather than later! These reminders weren't pushy; they were encouraging. Sometimes they would come in the form of easy conversation, or over email, through a note I left her, or even a text.

I found Tasha to be very receptive when I gave her time and didn't rush her into a conversation. Now, this was definitely not easy. It took patience, consideration, and paying attention to her non-verbal communication. Although she wasn't speaking with her mouth, her non-verbal behaviors screamed loudly. This included her facial expressions, body posture, expressions, the way she sat on the couch, etc. She might start with her legs turned away from me, but gradually they would move closer, until we were touching. I realized that she was opening up without saying a thing, and that words were soon to follow!

Be patient and sincere by providing gentle reminders, showing your spouse that their communication is important to you.

2. Create a Safe Space

When you are in a relationship and the other person doesn't communicate in the way you expect, it can be very frustrating. I know. I can recall times when my wife would finally open up to have a conversation after a day or so. And I would be fuming, upset, and irritated. I would be thinking, "Why did she waste all this time? We could have talked yesterday!" I was impatient! I soon discovered this was actually working against me. It would cause more tension and create an environment that wasn't healthy for communication.

It was vitally important that I created a safe space for Tasha to open up to me. When we become frustrated, angry, or upset, it can often push the other individual away. They might even shut back down. You have to remember that it might take a little longer to finally get to a place of verbal communication, and you don't want to create an environment that's not conducive to healthy sharing. Come to the conversation with the ability to hold your tongue and have the heart to listen without adverse commentary. You'll discover that more open conversation is shared when there is uninterrupted communication.

3.   Use "We" not "You"

My wife and I would often sit down and talk about our differences in communication style. I would highlight some of the things that I believed were most effective and how she needed to adjust. Often, I pointed out how "you" need to do this and how "you" need to do that. I had to realize that there wasn't necessarily a right or wrong way with either of our communication styles, but rather an effective way of merging them to create the way that worked for us.

Quite often we focus our attention on the other person's

inabilities and start pointing the finger. I had to move from talking about "you" and start using "we." This change focused on how we could achieve unity in communication and shifted attention to togetherness. I never wanted her to feel that when we finally sat down and communicated, it was all about her inabilities. I positioned the conversation in a way that focused on the importance of our collective effort! The conversations shifted from what "you" need to do better, to things that "we" could both improve upon. It shifted the attention to our goals, vision, dreams, and the most effective communication style to achieve them. It uncovered what was working for "us" and the behaviors we could modify.

If you are frustrated with your level of communication, try to change your language in conversation to reflect "we." Setting the focus on the goals of the relationship re-centers the conversation and allows both parties to work together to achieve a model marriage.

Common Pitfalls for Highly Communicative People

Not only did I discover keys in achieving effective communication with my wife's style, but I also unearthed things to avoid in using my own:

1.   **Uncalculated Conversations**

When my wife and I married, she realized that she had a spouse who loved to communicate and was always open for conversation. She often would ask me my opinion on things and I would readily respond. She would inquire about my thoughts on a certain subject and want to know my feelings, and I would easily pour them out for her to hear. But there were also times when we would be in a disagreement and she would shut down but I would continue to "communicate." Some of you reading this book might have found yourself in this spot before. Your spouse is done talking or doesn't want to talk and you are determined to be heard anyway! I eventually learned that although it was good to be so open to communication, it was important for my conversations to be calculated. What do I mean by calculated? Let me explain.

Just because you are an eager and a willing communicator, it doesn't necessarily mean that everything needs to be voiced. In the heat of the moment you can allow your emotions to drive the conversation and end up saying things that you regret. If you're not careful, it's pretty easy to shift from "communicating" to unloading or dumping on the other individual. Although those words you are speaking might describe your sentiments in that given moment, they don't reflect the totality of your feelings for your spouse. You can't always say what you feel! Feelings change. Releasing uncalculated words in conversation can feel good at the time, but can cause long-term damage to the relationship. You must ask yourself, "If I say this, what will it accomplish?" "How will this make them feel?" "Could this potentially cause more harm than good?"

I learned early in the relationship that our words carry power. Once, in the first year of our marriage, I was quite frustrated with our level of communication and the effort I was seeing from my wife. She wasn't opening up and talking quickly enough, and I had simply had enough. I was ready to just unload and let her know what I really thought about her maturity in the relationship. I was tired of being patient and understanding, and I was going let her have it! I told my wife in a disgusted tone of voice, "You're not ready for marriage…you're just not ready." And my wife looked back and me and said, "Maybe I'm not…" And every time we got into a disagreement or failed at effective communication, she would remind me of what I said: "Remember what you said; maybe I'm not ready for marriage."

The words that we speak are powerful. The Bible lets us know that life and death are in the power of our tongue. In marriage, it's possible to say something uncalculated in the heat of the moment, and it haunts us for the next 10 years. These words can cause emotional damage, unforgiveness, bitterness, and drive a wedge into the relationship. They become seeds of discord. The words that you speak out of your mouth take root in the relationship, and you start to reap the fruit of what you said. Things like: "You just are no good", I should just go ahead and leave this relationship, If you don't want to treat me right, there are many guys/women out there who would love to, You aren't sexy anymore like you used to be." All of these words carry weight, and when they are released, they can never be taken back. Uncalculated conversations and stinging words go through your partners' ears and are harbored within their hearts.

Start speaking good things over your relationship! Start speaking life into your marriage! Things might look bad and you might feel a certain way, but speak the opposite. Your spouse might be as opened as you like, but start encouraging them: "Baby, I appreciate your effort in communication; it's getting better!" Avoid negativity. Calculate the conversation so that it plants positive seeds into the relationship. Encouragement strengthens your partners desire to be better in the area that may be lacking.

2. Improper Timing

I like to talk and expose issues as soon as possible. This can be a good thing in some cases, but it can also be harmful. I had to learn that although what I was saying might be right, the timing could be totally wrong. Some of you can empathize; when you are ready to talk, you are ready to talk! You want to get it out. You want to get it off your chest. You want to have the conversation and be heard whether it's late at night, early in the morning, right after a long day at work, or when things are going perfectly fine in the relationship. You blindside your spouse! I learned that although communication is necessary, timing is essential.

Figuring out the right time and space is imperative. I discovered that my wife can get bored with the same scenery or with mundane repetition. So, having a conversation at home in the same space we last had a disagreement might not be the best location. Or, after a long day of multitasking, being brought into a conversation without warning can be too much. Early in the marriage I had to learn and value the use of strategic timing, finding the best times and places where my wife could feel comfortable to open up and freely converse. I found that instead of conversing at home, I could setup a lunch date. It was a different vibe. It was a different conversation. It was fresh thoughts, vibrant energy, and a different perspective. Going out of town was very effective as well. Getting away from work and the weekly ripping and running had a positive effect on the level of conversation.

Some of you are accustomed to conversation patterns: the same place, around the same time, and in the same space. Change it up! Get creative. Be strategic and identify the right timing and space that will facilitate a different level of healthy sharing and conversation. What you gain during these times will foster the unity between you.

BALANCE REDEFINED

Another key area in marriage is balance. According to dictionary.com, balance is defined as "an even distribution of weight enabling someone or something to remain upright and steady." It also says balance is "a condition in which different elements are equal or in the correct proportions." Although simple on paper, when applied in the context of a marriage or relationship, achieving balance often becomes very challenging. Each person comes to the table with various issues and commitments that capture some of their time and energy. Whether these are their personal goals, dreams, aspirations, hobbies, or day-to-day duties, inevitably these can take time away from their focus on the relationship. Many people enter marriage thinking their everyday lives will be like the honeymoon, where you can sleep-in together and gaze into each other's eyes all throughout the day. The reality is that our attention must be divided among many duties and responsibilities. Nobody wants a relationship where it seems like they are secondary to a job, a work schedule, homework, hobbies, children, or other friends and relationships. Where there is ineffective balance and perspective, it creates unnecessary weight and hardship in the marriage. All things might have a purpose and need attention, but how can you achieve them without losing your marriage? What is true balance, and what does it look like?"

In this section, we want to provide insight on the concept of balance. Like many of you, balance was a challenge for us in the beginning. It was challenging to the point that we didn't know if our marriage was strong enough to navigate through each other's schedules and obligations. It seemed like everything else was consuming our time, leaving little time for us to share. Through time and over the course of our marriage, we learned and applied some valuable lessons, giving us the stability needed for a successful marriage. We soon came to understand that balance wasn't necessarily what we initially thought. Before we describe to you our understanding of balance, we want to share a quick list of what balance is not:

3 Myths Regarding Balance

- Everything will receive equal time & attention
- Everything will always be in harmony
- Balance doesn't involve sacrifice

Throughout our relationship, God has allowed us to understand balance in a way we hadn't seen before. We define balance as follows:

Balance is the God-centered ability to effectively understand the need to fulfill a certain task or goal in a time or season, using collective effort.

Let's break it down. Each of the components in this definition is essential to achieving balance.

God at the Center

Many times, we aim to achieve goals and various aspirations in our own strength. Often, we wonder why what we want has not fully been achieved or realized. These unfulfilled dreams are often a direct result of us becoming the captain of our own destinies. We believe it is imperative that God is the head of each of our life's affairs. Having God at the forefront allows us to gain a true understanding of our purpose. Once purpose is garnered, it allows us to understand where to direct our focus and energies. Where should you be spending your time? What projects should you be working on? What things or people deserve your attention? In marriage, it's no longer just an individual focus, but there is the involvement of another person. So, although we have our individual purposes, God graces marriages with a collective purpose. These purposes are only revealed by God.

Every good thing is not a God thing. It was early in our marriage. We were just getting settled in as husband and wife and parents of two small children when a career opportunity arose that would allow our income to nearly triple. While we prayed about wanting more, we didn't fully understand how this would manifest. Matthew applied for a major position and received the call for the interview. We traveled to North Chicago and went through a series of interviews from morning until evening. The recruiter called and made us aware that both the supervisors and CEO were greatly impressed with his performance during the interviews, and we were instructed to wait on the final decision. We were confident that the position was an answered prayer. During the interview, the CEO advised Matthew of the time commitment and dedication that would be required for a successful career in the position. Although this was a bit alarming, we decided that we would work it out once the position was officially offered. However, as weeks passed, we got a call and learned that Matthew was not offered the position. We were devastated! We had already started to adjust our lives like the position had been attended.

Nearly a year later, we finally came to terms with the decision. We later learned, that had Matthew been offered the position, it would have had an adverse impact the growth and maturity of our union. Though we desired the increased income, we were not yet stable enough in the relationship to handle all the components of this opportunity. It was a good idea, but not in God's timing!

In order to achieve balance in your relationship, you must first understand whether what you are pursuing is God-centered. Also, you must discern whether what you are hoping to pursue is in proper timing. You might have a dream to go on a mission trip overseas; perhaps you have desired this since childhood. You are newly married and the opportunity arises, but it will cause you to be away from your husband and family the entire year. Although you should not neglect the dreams that God has given you, there must be calculated sensitivity of how this decision will work within the parameters of your relationship.

Is your relationship stable enough to handle being apart for even a month? Are all finances in place both for home and abroad? How will your children be in impacted? Will there be a better time to execute this vision? In a relationship, each decision must be God-centered and God-timed.

It takes a great level of maturity for true balance to occur. For instance, it may not be a missionary trip; maybe it's your two-day-a-week bowling league commitment, your monthly trip with the girls, or your weekly game nights with the fellas. It is important that each partner maintain their individual desires and routines, but also gain an understanding of how those desires ultimately impact the relationship. He's not jealous of your girls, and she's not hating on your homies, it's just important not to neglect the collective purpose of the relationship. It's the relationship between you and your spouse, that must always maintain priority status. And godly perspective must remain, especially when considering anything outside of this relationship.

Collective Effort

There will be seasons when large amounts of time and attention are needed in areas outside of the marriage. In order to maintain balance, one of the key factors that we found helpful is using collective effort. As mentioned above, each person will have desires, passions, and purposes that drive them. In a relationship, it is important that each partner is properly supported in each endeavor. While the goal is not to change the appetite or desire of the other individual, it is crucial that they become one in ensuring that the goal is realized. In a marriage, if individual goals or tasks are pursued individually (without the support of the spouse), it creates imbalance.

We want to share four different scenarios in our lives where collective effort in balance was necessary. In this section, we will discuss: running a business, having children, educational pursuits and handling ministry.

A. RUNNING A BUSINESS

It was early December and Matthew called me out of the blue. I was cradling the phone on my right shoulder, breastfeeding my son to the left, with my hands stretched across my computer's keyboard as I put the final touches on my exams and papers. I could hear his excitement, "Baby, you wouldn't believe the meeting I just got done with. I think we should do it!" "Do what babe, do what?!" I asked, "What are you talking about?" "I think we should take over ownership of this restaurant! It will only take so many thousands of dollars. We can withdraw that tomorrow and have a grand re-opening in a few weeks!!!" At this point, I thought I had married a lunatic! While we were both entrepreneurs, we had NEVER considered owning a RESTAURANT!

It was a decision that would require us to act within 48 hours. And while this tested the planner in me, I felt it was something worth exploring. Matthew came home with all the paperwork, we talked it out, and made the call. It was a go!

From the start, it was OUR business! I could have easily and justifiably said, "Hey babe, I will support you in every way, but this one is on you!" A fast food restaurant was never something we dreamed of doing; we had never talked about it; we never once considered it. Perhaps it was a subconscious dream of his that he'd never shared. Nevertheless, he was excited, and I immediately began to assess the contributions and level of input I could offer. Allowing him to take on this business venture alone could have caused an imbalance in our marriage and family. Functioning collectively means that although it might be an individual desire, it ultimately takes a collective effort.

Collective involvement and support were critical. While the time I could commit was minimal because I was preparing to defend my Master's thesis, I gave what I had. And while I wasn't the greatest fast food cook, I was good administratively. Immediately, I began to research the type of business structure that was most suitable for our new restaurant and printed and filed all the necessary paperwork. Then, I built our very first website. We hired a graphic designer to design our logo. I chose the uniforms and colors for our future employees and managers. Matthew hired a team of builders to replace the signage. I developed a job ad for necessary positions and publicized them. Our new business was in full effect! When we dropped our son off at daycare each day, we spent a majority of the time at the restaurant, gearing up for the upcoming grand re-opening! It was amazing! Soon, things began to come together. I could hardly believe it; just like that, we were restaurant owners.

Had I allowed Matthew to run this business alone, it would have been disastrous for our union. We were newly married, and time together was essential to the growth of what we hoped to build. Although Matthew was skilled in multiple areas, I was more proficient in important areas outside the kitchen. For three years we owned and operated a successful business that was geared towards employing hard-to-hire individuals. As Human Resources Manager and Chief Financial Officer, I interviewed and hired all staff and maintained accurate books for the duration of the business. Although it started as an aspiration of Matthew's, without our joint efforts, the business would have suffered.

It is important to consider this: In what areas could you involve yourself to create better balance in your marriage? If he is the basketball coach, I know you aren't that into sports, but you must be willing to at least come and pass out snacks. Can you help motivate the kids on the court? If practice is twice a week, can you attend at least one? We hope you get the picture. It is critical to maintain a collective effort in your individual pursuits. Otherwise, the time you are absence creates a space that eventually can cause the union to slowly grow in opposing directions.

B. HAVING CHILDREN

We were married in October of 2006. Our son was born in September of 2007. Yes, your calculations are right, I got her pregnant that December. LOL! While we both wanted children, we didn't have a family growth plan. In less than a year we would shift from learning what it meant to be man and wife to learning what it meant to be parents. Like many of you, we were advised in various manners to enjoy each other, travel, accomplish your life goals, and *then* have children. And while we partly agreed, God had a different plan. Although children are a blessing, they can become a major focal point of the relationship, creating challenges in maintaining effective balance. There are strategies that we implemented to maintain a loving marriage while learning the ropes of parenthood. Tasha breastfed both of our children the first year of their lives and they were very attached to her. There were times when I would be left alone with our children, and they had not yet adjusted to the bottle. Oh, what an experience that was! They wanted their Momma! Although this was difficult at times, it didn't excuse me from being a parent. I would often assist in other areas until they were weaned off the breast and onto the bottle. This included cooking, cleaning, and other chores. When the babies would cry late at night or in the wee hours of the morning, I couldn't do much, but I would often roll over and get up with her just for support. I had to remain conscious that I was out of the house most of the day while she was in the house all day, and I created opportunities for balance, where she could go out without the kids or just get a break.

Children are a wonderful addition to a family. I've heard it all! In some marriages, after the kids come, marriage is not the same. The focus is no longer on the adults, but shifts solely to the wellbeing of the new life. While we believe children can change the dynamics in marriage, they should never alter the bond. Some marriages lose their identities, lose their passion, and forfeit their purposes once kids arrive. However, kids were never meant to be a burden to a covenant marriage, but an added blessing.

How to Create Balance with Children in Marriage

1. Create frequent opportunities to strengthen the family bond

Impromptu vacation getaways, cultural enrichment opportunities, museums, aquarium visits, plays, concerts, movies, dining out, and collective worship opportunities all help with making memories and strengthening the collective family bond outside of day-to-day schedules.

2. Create opportunities where the children are the focal point

Here the focus can be children's extracurricular activities: dance, sports camps, or study skills practice. Take each child out on dates where it's just one parent and one child. Ultimately, the goal is achieving uninterrupted time where child is the focus. However, there must be a collective effort from both parents in various roles. If not, there is an imbalance. If only the mom helps with homework, there creates an imbalance and ultimately a burden on her. If Dad is always the one taking them to soccer practice, it is important to offer to share the load. The frustration and burden can be alleviated if there is a collective effort.

3. Maintain marriage moments

Utilize trusted individuals to help with childcare and development. This is more than obtaining an occasional sitter; this takes an intentional effort to ensure that your marriage doesn't become stale. Making these efforts helps even your children learn to respect and understand the love shared between their parents. When we prayed for the model marriage, we wanted to be models for our own children as well. Though there are more dynamics to consider, it is essential to establish time as a couple outside of the presence of children.

Building a family should never cause frustration or burden to a marriage. On the contrary, adding children creates an opportunity to creatively explore new ways to maintain and grow the love and memories that arise from a healthy family unit. *Having children and creating a family shouldn't mean forfeiting a healthy marriage*.

C. EDUCATIONAL PURSUITS

Before we were married, my wife was in graduate school. One month after our wedding she completed a Master of Arts degree. Then immediately she started her process to complete her Ph.D. She was extremely motivated with school. However, with building a family, her educational pursuit was a bit of a challenge. Despite this, I was in total support of her academic success. Those who are familiar with the research process understand that it can be quite intense. When my wife started the research process, she had to compile a literature review that took countless hours of research at the library, at home, and on campus. There were countless meetings between her and her advisors devising a research strategy. She had to travel and spend seemingly endless hours in the archives collecting data to ensure she presented sound research. Throughout the process, there were myriad deadlines that created heightened levels of stress and urgencies.

There were countless late nights and sometimes she would spend 24 hours at a time working, not getting any sleep and sometimes never coming to bed. Many of the activities we did for leisure were compromised. We decided to sit down and have a detailed conversation about how to effectively partner and see the successful completion of this degree. I had to come to grips with the idea of balance, and how balance didn't necessarily mean an equal distribution of time. Rather, balance was constructed around the God-centered demands of a given season. This was her pursuit, but this was also *our* pursuit. Although I was not part of the research process, my heart's desire was to see her successfully finish. This meant balancing our lives around this God-given focal point. I knew it wouldn't last forever, but I knew that it would have a great impact on every part of our lives for the next 18 months. Hence, I did everything in my power to lighten my wife's load during this time. Sometimes this meant preparing gourmet dinners and succulent desserts which I would bring to her office upstairs in our home, or to campus. There were days where I would pick our children up from school and keep them out until bedtime, so my wife could have the entire house to herself. I sent encouragement reminders via card, text, and phone call. I reminded her that we were in it together and she was doing a great job. I wanted to vocalize my support as well as provide tangible evidence of my love and support. Sometimes I would just sit with my laptop next to hers. I would just surf the internet, but my physical presence would offer moral support. As she advanced in the process, there were days she would totally detach from research. During these times, we would take weekend getaways, or see a movie, or go out to eat. These hiatuses motivated her to refresh and recalibrate and complete the research process.

I never wanted our collective goal of marriage and family to be an excuse or a hindrance as to why she didn't accomplish her personal pursuits.

While I was pursuing my Ph.D., Matthew was encouraged to continue his own education. He applied to a few graduate departments and initially it was denied admittance. While we were both devastated about this news, God knew best. Understanding balance, there was no way we could successfully pursue graduate degrees and properly support one another during the process.

However, as I was ending my Ph.D. process, Matthew applied to another graduate program and was admitted. Because I then knew the keys for successful completion and support, it was prime opportunity for me to reciprocate the very intentional love and support that Matthew displayed during my own process. Even our individual educational pursuits illustrate balance. This tag team approach was instrumental in helping us maintain a balanced life while successfully supporting one another to complete our individual goals.

Of course, it wasn't fun neglecting sleep, or not being able to go out, but we were in it together. We were each other's support. Anybody that wanted to add to that was like the icing on the cake. We refused to allow pride or selfishness to interrupt everything we sought to establish. At that end of it all, we could both say we were Doctors, a challenging but rewarding accomplishment was only attained through collective effort.

D. MARRIAGE & MINISTRY

One of the first challenges in our marriage related to ministry. Matthew was an avid and active leader at his brother's church and from the start of our relationship, we knew that ministry was to be an essential component of our union. While some of you may not be directly involved in ministry (specifically in the local church), our experience provided some key principles to help us maintain a sense of balance.

Over the years we have heard how, in many relationships, the wife would attend church but the husband would not. Or how the wife would be actively involved in areas of the local church and the husband would be uninvolved. This is a particularly dangerous imbalance in a marriage. It is vitally important that each spouse understand the importance of God and the necessity of collective worship. This opportunity reinforces the covenant and establishes God as priority.

Discovering Gift Mix:

We decided from the beginning of our relationship that we would attend church and actively participate together. Matthew spent countless hours at church doing the work of the ministry. From leadership, to planning, to music, to community outreach - his hand was in everything. Although I was active in ministry as well, I didn't have as many commitments and obligations. Early in our marriage he would spend time at the church for many hours, arriving home late, sometimes altering our plans. We had to find more effective ways to do ministry together. An important method was understanding our individual gift mix. I didn't feel the pressure to be who he was, but to develop into the fullness of who God called me to be individually. For example, I didn't sing in the choir or play a church instrument, but I began to cultivate my gift of dance, which wound up being a vital component to the music ministry. Dance was something I always did for pure enjoyment and entertainment, and now I was able to point that passion towards a purpose in God. As time went on, Matthew's passion was more pastoral and focused on leadership training. And though he was a minister, he never lost sight of the fact that before ministry, he was a husband and father. This balance was important to our union. Soon, I was also ordained as a minister and was being used in prophetic teaching alongside prayer and intercession. Understanding our specific passions within ministry helped create better balance in our marriage. We began to understand our individual identities in God while walking together in unity to fulfill purpose. In addition to our spiritual walk, we implemented some very practical principles. We came to church together and though our responsibilities at church varied after church, we left together as well. Matthew would have leadership meetings and rehearsal, sometimes after a long service. I waited (and not always patiently!) to ensure we left together. Later, when I became a member of the finance team, Matthew would have to take the kids and keep them at bay and wait until I was finished. Our commitment to balance would ultimately benefit our marriage.

As a wife, you might be reading this and desire for your husband to be as active at church as you are. It is important to understand that each individual has a specific gifting that must be uncovered. Assisting your spouse to find their placement in God and the local church creates unity in the marriage.

A husband might be reading this and feel the pressure of being involved at the level your wife is involved. You may never usher, sing in the choir, or be a part of the outreach team. But to create balance, it is important that you uncover your God-given purpose so that you both can function in your respective areas of ministry together.

It's Never a Competition

It's natural to want the best for yourself. However, in marriage it's important to know that what you each do individually is ultimately a representation of the other. Hence, when you operate in the same industry, it's easy to develop an unhealthy sense of competition. In marriage, you are on the same team, and it becomes even more important to openly and actively support one another and understand the parameters of each other's assignments.

In the age of social media, you should be the first one loving, liking, and sharing each other's posts. It is critical to understand that your public show of support provides a sense of protection and reinforces unity. Also, providing genuine compliments to your spouse provides a level of affirmation that is often more powerful than from any other source. *It's important to understand that your spouse needs your approval, even if he or she is not seeking it.*

Lastly, understanding the parameters of each other's assignments enables you to properly support your spouse. For example, if your spouse was called for a speaking engagement and you too are a dynamic speaker, accept that this time you aren't on the program and the only thing required of you is to assist your spouse in successfully fulfilling their task. This is done most effectively through intercession and remaining flexible and available where needed. The ability to balance your own gift while supporting your spouse is both powerful and commendable.

Leaving Church at Church

Because ministry was an essential component of our lives, it was very easy to integrate its demands in our home. Even if it's not church, this principle can be applied to other areas of life as well. We made intentional efforts to leave church at church. When we were at church we would give 100% and were fully present. However, once we were home, we made a concerted effort to focus only on things that impacted our marriage and family.

At first, we found ourselves discussing church situations and occurrences but would have to discipline ourselves and respect the necessary separation of church life and home life. Many relationships suffer because church is integrated within marriage, and marriage is integrated with work, etc. We can become so programmed to certain places and obligations that we lose sight of the value of uninterrupted time and focus at home. The struggles and stresses of work are brought home, which creates an environment not conducive to a healthy marriage. Further, this can lead to inward struggles while neglecting the needs of one's family and spouse.

DRS. MATTHEW & LATASHA NESBITT

ஜ

5 KEYS TO MAINTAINING A FRESH
&
THRIVING MARRIAGE

Before we conclude this chapter on marriage we want to provide you with 5 keys that we utilized to maintain a fresh and thriving marriage. Once you are married for a while, marriage has the potential to become mundane and dull. This doesn't necessarily mean you are growing apart or any love is lost, but this is a great indicator that the marriage must be intentionally cultivated. If you haven't yet reached this phase it marriage, don't be surprised when it comes. Instead of allowing the union to continue operating on this level, we've discovered 5 critical ways to keep things fresh. If you haven't already implemented some of these, we recommend giving them a try!

1. Cultivating Environments

For a marriage to continue to grow and thrive, it must be cultivated in the correct environments. Just as a plant or a tree, it needs the proper sunlight, water, and nutrients present to ensure it continues to grow properly. Without these, it begins to wither, and many times dies. These environments must be first conducive to one's individual growth. One of the biggest mistakes in marriage is becoming too comfortable, complacent, and casual. We get so excited and happy at the notion of getting married, but don't realize that the work really starts after the ceremony. *Anybody can get married, but everybody won't stay married.* Marriage takes continual growth, not only collectively but individually. You must ask yourself the questions, "What am I doing to become a better husband?" or "In what areas can I mature to become a better wife?" One common misconception is to think that you came into the marriage with everything needed to sustain it. We believe that you have the necessary tools in your tool box, but they must be sharpened and consistently tested to remain cutting-edge and effective. Doing what you did five years ago might not be relevant in the relationship today. Relationships evolve. And if you aren't willing to invest the proper time and attention to personal growth, it will have a direct effect on the sum total of the relationship.

Some of the environments that we found to be very helpful in personal growth and development are conferences and retreats. We've done women's conferences that are focused on empowering the whole woman, and conferences that challenge growth through discovering one's personal identity and purpose in life. We have also invested in women's conferences that give strategies on how to become a more effective wife, and those that offer an opportunity to hear testimonies of women who have experienced success in marriage. We have taken advantage of men's conferences that promote the total man - conferences that illuminate places of healing and deliverance and shine light on things that come to hold men down, revealing common pitfalls that men face in marriage. We have profited so much individually from being in these environments and being able to obtain new knowledge that would be applicable to our own marriage. Never think you know it ALL! ***Exposure to new information and concepts can revolutionize your marriage.***

We also think it is important to attend various workshops, retreats, and conferences together. This often is a great opportunity to spend time together without children, and just be refreshed.

In a marriage, you can often find yourself devoting energy to many places and things, whether it's time at your job, your schooling, children, church, career, or various day-to-day tasks. It is necessary to make sure that you have periods where you aren't giving out, but simply receiving. This was a huge adjustment for us! We were so accustomed to serving, helping, or planning that we often didn't know how to just come, receive, and leave! ***Married couples that always are giving out and have no places to just receive often become burnt out and bankrupt.*** We had to learn the value of coming into spaces and being poured into and refreshed and not to let burn-out become the standard of the relationship. We had to learn when we were about hit this space in the relationship and find environments that could revitalize and strengthen the love that we shared.

Lastly, being around other thriving and healthy relationships can be quite refreshing. We found ourselves going out to dinner and being in spaces with couples and married people who were excelling in their relationships. You try it! Take a night and spend it with a couple who is really in love and passionate about each other. When they hold hands, kiss, show signs of affection, talk sweetly, and have genuinely sweet interactions, it's impossible to be hard, crusty and staunch around them! Their love and affection rubs off on you. You find yourself holding hands and you haven't held hands in years! LOL. It sparks something, puts the twinkle back in your eyes, and you end the night on a high note when you get back home! Finding yourself in the right environment can be everything!

2. Spontaneous Love

Another way to keep things fresh in the relationship is to exhibit spontaneous expression of love. Think about it. God willing, you are going to be married to your spouse for a long, long time. You are going to have interactions with them daily and will be living life with them forever. One of the great failures in any relationship is boring redundancy and predictability. Although this can be beneficial in certain areas of the relationship, it can become very frustrating in others. Early in the relationship we fell on the floor laughing about Valentine's Day! We thought it was comical the way people go out and get their cards, stuffed teddy bears, chocolates, roses, or big ol' basket wrapped in cellophane to show love on a prescribed day. We respected the idea that love was acknowledged, but we disliked the overcompensation associated with one day being set aside to express one's love for another. Why can't it be weekly, or monthly, or sporadic throughout certain times of the year?

If your marriage is going to stay fresh, you have to exhibit expressions of love outside of prescribed days like birthdays, anniversaries, and holidays. Although these days should be made special, they shouldn't be the only days where effort is exerted for gifts and acknowledgement. We once blocked off an entire week for special gifts and expressions of love. We showered each other. Other times we have turned our house into a spa, lit candles all around the tub and giving manicures and pedicures, hot baths, and oil massages. You don't even have to spend a lot of money. Often a spouse's thoughtfulness, time, energies, and creativity can go further than what money can buy. What makes your spouse happy? What makes them feel special? Are they more driven by gifts and presents or do they love time spent together or words written in an extended card or letter? We had to discover what flips each other's switch and find ourselves spontaneously thinking of things that would light the match of love and affection! Be creative. Do some research. Don't rush and throw things together. Give it some thought and ensure that your spouse knows that they are always on your mind.

Lastly, we made a rule early in our marriage that we would have frequent intimacy! Yep! Getting it in and SEXIN'!' We are firm believers that the more, the better! We never wanted to be in a marriage that left either partner unfulfilled when it came to sexual intimacy. Everything that your wife or husband can dream of should happen right in your bedroom! There should never be a time when the other's sexual needs are not being met. Now there will be times when schedules are hectic, and with other obligations things can seem a bit strained. Sometimes you'll have a heightened level of stress, tension, and pressure around the house. It doesn't necessarily mean that something is wrong, but life sometimes takes its toll on your ability to fully connect. Someone has to close the gap. Someone has to initiate and end the drought! Intimacy can make a huge difference in the vibe and on the interactions in your marriage. Also, don't be afraid to try some new things and discover what works best for you both. Boy, do we have some stories…but I think we'll stop here! ☺

3. Spending time together with God

It is important to understand that your marriage must have a foundation that that is built on God. Many people include God in the sacredness of their ceremony when lighting candles and going through the vows, but neglect Him after the ceremony is over. A marriage that doesn't include God is one that relies on natural strengths and abilities and neglects the infinite ability of God.

From the start of our relationship, we knew that God had brought us together and acknowledged that it would take Him to keep us together. Therefore, we established God as priority in the relationship and found it important to spend time together with Him. We make it a point to leave for church and attend service together. We find it very refreshing to worship together, as this softens our hearts toward Him and toward one another. If you have been married for a while, you know all about riding to church and having a disagreement on the way there! But worshiping, hearing the Word, and wholeheartedly seeking God somehow changes everything. If you do it sincerely, it's impossible to go into service upset and leave the same way. When entering the presence of God, things happen - things change! God refocuses your attention and provides you with conviction, clarity, and a pliable heart to want to please Him. This has a direct result on your marriage and interactions with your spouse. That's why we highly recommend that married couples attend church and worship together. One partner sleeping in or washing the car, or even working during these times really has an impact on the unity in the home. Everybody is not receiving. Everybody is not on the same page. And in order to establish the culture of honoring God through worship, it's important to have unity in this area.

We have also found it to be very helpful to pray together at home. We all know that schedules can get busy and our lives become hectic. Finding time to pray together can start well, but soon fade and start to dwindle away. Scheduling intentional times to pray together is very important. We have found that mornings are most effective for us. We come together and acknowledge God, asking Him to direct us, lead us, guide us, and continue to provide us with the grace to be successful in every area of our life. It doesn't have to be deep and drawn out. As you both roll over and wake up, grab hands and take turns with a brief prayer. This helps us to start the day off unified and lets the enemy know he can't get in between us and that we are connected. This is powerful. Too often arguments, disagreements, disgruntlements, and anger can fester and simmer so long until there comes a boiling point in the house and things blow up. One of the strategies to prevent blow-ups is implementing prayer times so that each heart is pliable and open to healthy communication. Often God will provide wisdom, understanding, and direction needed to navigate through whatever problems you might be facing. Neglecting prayer and time with God is a major tactic used by the enemy to keep your marriage divided. You should try it! The next time there is tension in your marriage, just stop and ask your spouse to join together in prayer. Allow God to intervene in all of your affairs and watch the difference that this makes.

At various times of the year we also come together for periods of fasting. We establish a focal point during this time and seek God together. Usually this happens toward the close of the year. We also fast together for shorter periods monthly or bimonthly. We typically set aside days or even weeks to turn away our plates. This allows us to re-center our attention on God and earnestly seek his wisdom on things pertaining to our life and family. We have witnessed how this has kept a certain spiritual climate in our home. It allows our marriage to stay energized and fueled with the Holy Spirit's leading. It also reinforces the promises of God, while keeping a blood hedge around us. The enemy can't stand it when a relationship is united with prayer and fasting.

4. Change of Scenery

In our marriage, we have learned that a change of scenery can work wonders. For so many years we lived in a small college town in Illinois. Although we enjoyed family and friends and the quaintness of the community, we would often become bored with the scenery and options available for married couples. Before kids it seemed like we had most of our weekends free. We would try to maximize our time together, while getting to know each other and sharing our love. Most of the time this would consist of dinner at a very nice place, going to the mall, or heading to the movies! It got to where we were almost "regulars" at some of our favorite places to eat, because the options of fine dining were so few. They knew what we liked to order, where we liked to sit, and our favorite wait staff. We would make our rounds at the mall, starting at Macy's, and frequenting Express for him, and Ann Taylor &

TJ Maxx for her. And if a really good movie came out, we were guaranteed to run into the entire community at the late show! In order to avoid frustration with where we were at the time, we decided to make some conscious decisions for the better of our relationship.

We decided that once a month, we would travel somewhere regionally. At the time this meant Chicago, St. Louis, Indianapolis, or places that were within three to four hours' driving distance. We would leave Friday during the day and find a reasonable hotel for an overnight stay. We would have an amazing date night planned for that Friday and explore the city, doing fun activities or shopping on that Saturday. It was so refreshing! We worked hard during the week, had responsibilities with our educational pursuits, business, ministry, and kids; these getaways were much needed! This would give us time away from our typical environment so that we could get away briefly to just breathe. Many of you of you are probably saying, "What about the kids?" Half the time we took them with us and the other half we left them with family. There's nothing wrong with getting away as a family, but taking dedicated time to just enjoy each other is important as well. Ensuring that the entire family is refreshed can also have a major impact on the marriage. What good does it do to go away and things are out of order with your kids? You'll never achieve the rest, relaxation, or enjoyment anyway. Why not take them and expose them to new scenery as well, and the whole family can come back recharged?

If your marriage is going to stay fresh and thrive, you have to change it up and be intentional about it! We would schedule these weekends so that our sanity wasn't compromised. They didn't take a lot of money and proved to be a necessary part of our peace and happiness.

We also implemented that twice a year, we would travel more extensively for a week or so, out of the country. This would be separate from ministry travel or vacations with the kids. We have had some amazing experiences in places like Mexico, various places throughout the Caribbean, Hawaii and more. We typically stay at a resort and explored! We participated in excursion tours, riding bikes, eating local food, and snorkeling! These prove to be great opportunities for connecting and giving us "honeymoon–like" feeling again. We often hear people in marriages say, "I don't have the time," or "We just don't have the money to do this." Keep this in mind: **When we neglect to properly invest into our relationship, it will ultimately come out on the back end, being more costly to the sanity of the marriage.** Stop making excuses and make your marriage a priority!

5. Revisiting Your Goals/Dreams

Marriages that operate with tunnel vision are those that struggle to accomplish major goals. Tunnel vision can mean that you and your spouse are so consumed with day-to-day living that you give no attention to each other's dreams. In marriage, it is very possible to get stuck in daily routines. These routines are often crowded with the essentials of life and finding ways to just maintain what you have established. We hear many couples explaining how a job has consumed all of their time. Or how things have shifted and their kids are their primary focus; or how they have put their goals on the back burner. And although we do understand the concepts of priorities and sacrifice, we also understand the possibility of having it all! Who said that you can't be a full-time working spouse and go back to school?! I know kids can be expensive, but who said you can't have kids and still save money? Why can't you have a super hectic schedule and still lose 50lbs this year? Your marriage will never stay fresh if you have the mindset of just managing and maintaining. You have to get out of that survival mode and create opportunities where you establish strategies to thrive. This often happens when you are frustrated with the dullness of life and want to create a new normal.

As you assess what you have in your relationship, ask yourself these questions:

- What are the goals of your marriage?
- Where are we pushing towards in this season of our lives?
- Where should our time and energies be exerted to gain the best results of this season?
- What is working and what is not?
- What are our one-year, five-year, and ten-year goals?
- Where do we see ourselves?

And if you haven't sat down and had real heart-to-heart discussions about these areas with your spouse, you are haphazardly moving in the marriage with a limited sense of direction. **Success in marriage just doesn't happen; it must be intentional.**

In our marriage, we have established the top of the year as a time of establishing our focus and creating goals and objectives for the year. Each year the marriage changes. The marriage evolves. The focuses of last year might have shifted into a totally different area. We typically sit down for 2-3 hours and talk about what we really sense God wants us to do each year. We also discuss things that we need to implement, things that must be adjusted or removed, and areas that need our undivided attention. In these times, we uncover the plans of God and some of things that we are passionate about achieving. If these times are not established for us to revisit our goals and dreams, they often will become neglected. Many marriages suffer because the passion and fire of their spouse has not received attention or hasn't been adequately voiced. Hearing and understanding the heart of your spouse allows what matters to them to be heard. In the previous chapter, we talked about the pursuit of Matthew's Ph.D. This was a voiced desire, and we established practical strategies and support systems to ensure this was achieved. If this desire was never revisited, it would have been a dream that was sidelined or neglected. ***One of the greatest opportunities in marriage is having an individual who is committed to partnering in your success.***

It's a team effort.

Mirror Moments

Questions

1. In what ways can you strengthen the relationship and create freshness?

2. Identify your communication style. Identify your spouse's communication style.

3. Name the top 3 areas of focus for your marriage, currently.

4. If you were missing from your marriage, what would be gone? If your spouse were missing what would be absent?

5. How often have you and your spouse spent time together in God (prayer, bible reading, fasting)?

Mirror Moments

Reflections

Mirror Moments

Reflections

Mirror Moments

Reflections

Mirror Moments

Reflections

CONCLUSION

From where we stand today, we can look back over our journey and see the importance of each phase. It was imperative to utilize each stage of our relationship – even before we were in relationship - to build a foundation for the next. Our singleness made us into whole people; it was the time when we had to examine ourselves and commit to focusing on God and who we were in Him. This readied us for dating, where we delighted to learn one another, and learn how we might complement each other and grow together. The engagement phase solidified our commitment to each other and made official our intention to navigate life together. And finally, in marriage we have become one, and in this phase, we use our life's lessons to build with one another, to love one another, and to lead our family.

Through each of these phases, with their ups and downs, through each serious moment and each celebratory one, it was imperative to always let God guide us, being the Lord of our rings. Our communication with God served as a thread that wove us together.

We've covered a plethora of areas in this book, as our goal was to share *our* experience. Whatever stage of relationship you are in, we hope that some of the principles shared will enlighten your journey. Of course, there are an array of areas involving relationships that we could have addressed, (i.e. divorce, step-parenting, infidelity, to name a few), however, we focused our attention on areas within our experience that proved successful. It is our hope you continue to grow and mature in your current relationship status. With God's help, you'll flourish in areas that once proved challenging.

Here, at the end of our contribution to your journey, we want to provide you with a prayer (see below) for each step of the way.

Wherever you are on your journey, let God steer – and enjoy the ride!

SINGLES PRAYER/DECLARATION
(read aloud)

Father, I thank You for the power to embrace my time of singleness. I pray that during this time You reveal areas of my life that require healing and restoration. As I go through this process, Lord remove all unhealthy soul ties that have kept me bound in my mind, will and emotions. I decree and declare that I am free from the burdens and weight of unhealthy and failed relationships of my past. I free myself from all shame and condemnation of past my mistakes and encounters. I am not bound by my past but now released into my future. I receive new thoughts, a sound mind, the power to wait, to have faith, and uncover the value of who You have made me. The plans and purposes of my life are uncovered NOW! I walk in new dimensions of confidence with anticipated success. New doors of opportunity are opening as You are readying me to embrace new relationships, new perspectives, new ideologies, new mindsets, and new habits. I receive new strategies of bringing order and wholeness to my life. I decree and declare that nothing is missing, lacking or broken in my life! I decree my finances are lining up with God's will for my life. I decree and declare that any educational pursuits, career advancements, business ventures, and/or contracts are no longer delayed, as I call for their release. I am Your child and I will begin to live the abundant life that You promised, NOW!

In Jesus' name, AMEN.

†

DATING PRAYER/DECLARATION

(read aloud)

Lord, I thank You for this stage of my life. As I am entertaining this stage of dating, I ask that you reveal if this is a God-ordained, long-standing relationship for my life. I thank You for giving me the power and the ability to put this relationship in proper perspective. Help me not to be fueled by my feelings, but refocused on my future. God, I thank you for new disciplines in this relationship. Help me to develop my standards and keep them. Help me not to settle for the sake of convenience. Help me to stay true to Your plan for dating relationships, maintaining my abstinence until marriage. Continue to reveal my identity and not allow it to be lost. Father, provide wisdom and don't allow me to take on a role of a spouse prematurely. If there are unsettled or unresolved relationships from my past, give me the strength to embrace true commitment and respect, in this relationship. Reveal the individuals assigned to my life that provide sources of accountability and trust; where I can be transparent about my relationship. Place people in my life that have the experience and wisdom to adequately support a strong foundation. Most importantly, Father, I place you at the center of my attention and first in my life. You said in your word, as I continue to seek You, all these things would be added unto me.

In Jesus' name, AMEN.

✝

ENGAGED PRAYER/DECLARATION

(read aloud)

Father, as I have entered into this first realm of marriage, I thank You that You are properly preparing me. I thank You that my patience is intact. I thank You for identifying the right mate that can handle the magnitude of my future in You. I dismantle every assignment of the enemy that is planned for this relationship. I break word curses that have been spoken by people about me and my mate. I disallow any seeds of discord, causing disunity to manifest. I decree and declare that this relationship shall be covered by You and flourish into a healthy marriage. I decree and declare that no weapon that is formed against me and my mate shall prosper and that a blood hedge of protection encamps around us. I decree and declare that the divine purpose of our relationship be revealed and that you will gird us up with wisdom for the days ahead. Father, give us supernatural favor with everything pertaining to our upcoming marriage. I declare and decree favor with the purchasing of wedding rings. I decree and declare favor on the day of the wedding and other preparations. I decree and declare favor with housing and living arrangements that are forth coming. I decree and declare special grace as we blend each sides of our families. Thank you that there is a free flow between us all. As we continue to seek your presence, grace us to handle the fullness of the assignments you have for us individually and especially collectively.

In Jesus' name, AMEN.

†

MARRIED PRAYER & DECLARATION

(read aloud with spouse)

Father, we thank You for our marriage and the covenant that has been established. We thank you God that our bond is unbreakable. Our marriage is precious to You as it is to us! Everything about it is worth fighting for! We cancel out plans of the enemy to cause divorce. We pray for heightened levels of discernment to illuminate areas of attack on our marriage.

We decree and declare greater levels of effective and efficient communication, creative and healthy ways to express ourselves.

We decree and declare that the spirit of poverty and lack do not reside within our marriage. We thank You that You are transitioning us from not enough, to just enough, to more than enough. We receive overflow!

We decree and declare that there are no breaches in covenant through infidelity, and pray revitalized levels of intimacy between each other. Our marriage is fresh and new.

We decree and declare that our children are not a burden but a blessing and that You are providing new strategies on how to balance our marriage with our children. We decree and declare that our gifts and talents are continuing to be revealed and thank You that You are cultivating our identities in ministry and in the marketplace.

Thank you, God, that what we spoke in our vows, is reflected within the climate of our home. Thank you Father that what we share in our marriage is one that can be modeled after, as we follow your leading.

In Jesus' name, AMEN.

MEET THE AUTHORS

Dynamic leader, profound speaker, and author of books such as *Lawbreaker* and *Vision Enhancer*, Matthew Nesbitt is also an itinerant minister. Matthew travels across the country building churches and communities through demonstration and power. His charismatic and relatable approach is building a legacy infused with love. Personal Site: DrMatthewnesbitt.com
Family site: www.nowwiththenesbitts.com

Dr. Nes's (Tasha) relevant and passionate teachings intertwine spiritual truths with practical application. She is the author of three works, and her repertoire of writing is widely circulated and growing quickly. Founder of Dr. Nes International (DNI), she motivates individuals and organizations to produce real results in their lives. In addition to this, DNI offers a range of literary publication services. Personal site: www.iamdrnes.com & Family site: www.nowwiththenesbitts.com.